CIVIL WAR GHOSTS OF NORTH GEORGIA

CIVIL WAR GHOSTS OF NORTH GEORGIA

JIM MILES

Haunted America

Published by Haunted America
A Division of The History Press
Charleston, SC 29403
www.historypress.net

All photos by author unless otherwise noted.

First published 2013

Manufactured in the United States

ISBN 978.1.62619.184.6

Library of Congress CIP data applied for.

Notice: The information in this book is true and complete to the best of our knowledge. It is offered without guarantee on the part of the author or The History Press. The author and The History Press disclaim all liability in connection with the use of this book.

For the latest members of the Miles family: Jeremy, Xavier and Emmett Barker.

CONTENTS

PREFACE

Over the past twenty-five years, I have spent a great deal of time prowling all the major, and most of the minor, Civil War battlefields in this country, all the while writing a multiple-volume historical tour guide series. I hate the crowds that swarm over the popular battlefields in the middle of the day, so I am often out at dawn and dusk, alone except for my wife, Earline, and she often sits in the car and reads while I traipse off into the fields and woods. ("Another battlefield," she once said. "I knew it. I saw the boring glow on the horizon.")

I find particular pleasure in lingering at the most storied sites in America's Civil War: the Hornet's Nest at Shiloh; Little Round Top, where my Alabama ancestors were sacrificed; The Angle at Gettysburg; Chickamauga's Snodgrass Hill; the Sunken Road at Antietam; the Railroad Cut at Second Manassas; Cheatham Hill at Kennesaw Mountain; the site of Jackson's flank attack at Chancellorsville; Spotsylvania's Mule Shoe; the Mine at Petersburg; and Surrender Field at Appomattox.

After reading all the accounts of ghosts inhabiting so many battlefields and interacting with so many witnesses, I paused to take stock. Had I ever encountered anything eerie? With regret, I concluded that I have never personally witnessed anything out of the ordinary. I wondered if perhaps I was not on a battlefield on the right day but was forced to reject that idea. I have been at Vicksburg, Shiloh, Chickamauga, Atlanta, Lookout Mountain, Stones River, Antietam, Gettysburg and Manassas, as well as other places, on the anniversaries of those battles. I have also spent many sunrises and sunsets at national and Confederate cemeteries but never felt uneasy. I fear I do not have the appropriate psychic makeup to witness such manifestations, and I suppose that is fortunate.

However, I am not finished with my Civil War work. There is still the chance of being challenged by a ghostly sentry, smelling the gun smoke and stench of death or watching an otherworldly reenactment. Maybe I will see Old Green Eyes at Chickamauga or James Longstreet's ghost in Gainesville. You never know.

So, what strange things have transpired at Georgia's Civil War sites? The phenomena seem to take two forms. The first are traditional ghosts, the alleged spirits of the dead that continue to haunt the places where they died, often suddenly and violently. These entities cannot accept the fact that they are dead and attempt to continue living their "lives" as they were at the time of death. Others seem to be searching for something, a loved one separated by death, a body part lost in combat, the answer to a question or perhaps forgiveness for a long-ago act.

The second type of paranormal experience seems to be a psychic recording of moments in a life already lived or a traumatic event. These movies out of time may be triggered by a date (often an anniversary), unusual atmospheric conditions, a time of day or night or simply by someone sensitive enough to accept the experience. These recordings are often accompanied by audio (usually muffled) and by scent (the smell of gun smoke and the cloying odor of death).

Predictably, Georgia's Civil War haunts correspond to significant military activity. Chickamauga, second only to Gettysburg in casualties, abounds with the strangest assortment of ghostly activity. The Atlanta Campaign features at several prominent psychically infested areas. A paranormal reenactment at the Hell Hole at New Hope Church was seen and smelled by two recognized Civil War experts. Antebellum houses in Athens retain their wartime residents. The old Augusta Arsenal, now Regents State University, hosts a plethora of ghosts. Georgia's greatest Civil War general, James Longstreet, haunts his rediscovered home in Gainesville. Other Civil War spirits remain in smaller cities and towns throughout northern Georgia. New sightings of wartime ghosts are regularly reported.

You may have visited the battle sites and read of Georgia's Civil War history. It is now time to discover the paranormal activity that regularly occurs at those storied places in north Georgia.

PART I
THE GHOSTS OF CHICKAMAUGA
THE RIVER OF DEATH

CHICKAMAUGA BATTLEFIELD

During the summer of 1863, William Rosecrans's Union Army of the Cumberland outflanked Braxton Bragg's Confederate Army of Tennessee and sent the Southerners reeling from central Tennessee into northern Georgia. Bragg stopped there and set a trap, reinforced by a corps from the Army of Northern Virginia under James Longstreet. The two-day struggle at Chickamauga resulted in the second-bloodiest battle of the Civil War and a tremendous Confederate victory that left Rosecrans staggering back to Chattanooga. In the Cherokee language, Chickamauga means "river of death," a terribly appropriate name.

This large battlefield has spawned many ghost stories. Although usually serene during the day, all psychic hell breaks loose after dark. At night, visitors and park rangers alike hear shots, screams and sounds of phantom men running and cavalry charging; have feelings of being watched; and see spectral figures fighting through the thick vegetation. Old Green Eyes prowls for more cadavers, and the Lady in White searches for her fiancé.

The Original Chickamauga Ghost Story

"Did you ever see a ghost?" he asked. "They used to see them on the Chickamauga battlefield just after the war." This first reported ghost from

Old Green Eyes, phantom infantry and spectral cavalry can be seen among Chickamauga's fields and woods each night as a mist settles across the battlefield.

the battlefield was sighted in 1876, as related by Jim Carlock, an early citizen of the Post Oak community, in Susie Blaylock McDaniel's *The Official History of Catoosa County*. Following a centennial celebration in Chattanooga, Carlock and several other men were riding in a wagon, while a man identified only as Mr. Shields rode alongside on a horse. That portion of the battlefield was deserted, with no houses, and they spotted a figure that measured ten feet in height and had a "big white head." For some unknown reason, Shields rode up to the apparition and hit it, which caused a baby to cry. The ghost, described as a black woman with a load of clothes balanced on her head, shouted, "Let me alone!"

Wild Phantom Cavalry

In the fall of 1976, near the anniversary of the battle, Buck Dugger was running an U.S. Army ROTC training program. Early one morning, he heard the sound of many horses approaching. "You could hear the horses; you could hear the breathing," he said. "You could hear them riding by, and what amazed us was that it was not an easy ride like someone riding through a tranquil park. It was someone riding hellbent for leather." He and his comrades assumed that there was a riding stable nearby and thought no more of it.

Twenty years later, Dugger was back at Chickamauga as a National Park Service (NPS) employee. He learned that there had never been stables in the area where he had heard the horses, but cavalry had been active there during the battle. He also heard other ghostly sounds. "When I was working up close where the trains area would be, the mixture of sounds included wagons and livery and other things, a lot of clanking sounds," he said. "We were along the battle line; it sounded like the hoofbeats were a lot faster, a lot harder."

Psychic Hotline

Late one night, Dugger was installing a new phone system in offices at the battlefield museum. The superintendent's telephone speaker came on "with a dial tone just blaring in his office," he related. When he turned it off, the speaker on the phone in the next office, that of the purchasing agent, activated. He also turned that off, but phones continued to ring in sequence

The Chickamauga Visitors' Center, where a ghost army once paraded past. Gremlins also infested a new telephone system.

until Dugger had made a circuit of the offices and had returned to his own. All was quiet for a second, but then his phone came on and he suddenly felt very strange. He determined that there had to be a rational explanation. "I'm sure that's what it is," Dugger said. "Because I still have to work here at night, so that's the only thing it can be because I don't believe in ghosts." Despite his rationalizing, the phones were not connected, so they could not have been activated in such a manner.

The Ghoul: Old Green Eyes

Famed ghost hunter Dale Kaczmarek conducted the first in-depth ghost research at Chickamauga. Edward Tinney, chief historian at the battlefield park and a World War II veteran who worked here from 1969 to 1986, told him the legend of Old Green Eyes. The preferred origin of that ghost is that it was a Confederate soldier whose body was destroyed by an artillery shell. Only his head was left to be buried, and it regularly bobs across the battlefield at night, particularly on Snodgrass Hill, moaning piteously while frantically searching for its body.

"History says ghosts in the battlefield such as the Green Eyes tale began happening soon after the war," Tinney said. One employee maintains that the beheaded soldier was a Confederate killed by his Federal brother.

An alternate theory is that Old Green Eyes is a ghoul, a supernatural corpse-eating creature predating the settlers, and perhaps even the Indians. Native American myths describe large, hairy creatures that would make off with children at night. Rumors persist that during lulls in Confederate attacks against Snodgrass Hill, the entity was seen inspecting the recently deceased, choosing the best for its feast. Many bodies were never recovered.

Whichever story you prefer, Old Green Eyes is Chickamauga's most frequently reported haunt, often seen around dusk—two big glowing eyes that approach the unwary, the creature groaning mournfully.

Tinney claimed that he was "not a superstitious man" but freely admitted, "I've seen Green Eyes. You know he's watching. We all know he's watching us. It's enough to make the hair stand up on the back of your neck."

Tinney encountered Old Green Eyes several times. He was hiking a park trail on a foggy night in 1976 when he had a close encounter with a human-like shape that was not human and came within twenty feet of him. "When it passed me," he told Richard Winer in 1981, "I could see his hair was long like a woman's. The eyes—I'll never forget those eyes—they were glaring, almost greenish-orange in color, flashing like some sort of wild animal. The teeth were long and pointed like fangs. It was wearing a dark cape that seemed to be flapping in the wind, but there was no wind. I didn't know whether to run or scream or what."

Tinney was out early that morning, 4:00 or 5:00 a.m., on the anniversary of the battle, walking along a park road to check on reenactment groups camped on the grounds. "As I was walking down, the moon was still out, and you could see just the same as daylight. I noticed someone coming toward me. I thought it might be one of the reenactors but not knowing for certain I moved over to the other side of the road and the closer it came the more apprehensive I get. Because it didn't look normal. It didn't look human."

When just a few feet away, "It turned to me. I turned to it. When it turned to me, it began to smile." The grin on its face, Tinney stated, "said drop dead." As soon as they passed each other, a car came around the bend, headlights blazing through the fog. Tinney walked backward to keep an eye on the figure, which "never looked back at me. After it got parallel with me, it looked forward, and it just kept looking up the road. It dissipated, it vanished. What happened to it?" The creature did not cross the road to his side, as he would have seen it. It did not go into the woods on the other side because the underbrush was impenetrable. "Now where did he go?" Tinney asked. He did not know what it was, but it was definitely not of this world.

"Whatever this was had to be alive at one time because it walked," he thought. "This walked, just like you and I." Other witnesses swear that if the apparition makes eye contact, it will stare a person down until it passes out of sight. "Wherever there has been great suffering," Tinney said, "people are always seeing strange things."

Dead Man's Battlefield

Ranger Charlie Fisher never saw Old Green Eyes, but he attributed two separate one-car wrecks in the park during the 1970s to drivers distracted by the creature. Both cars struck the same tree. The monster has been spotted briefly by several rangers on night patrol, the green eyes passing in front of their vehicles and disappearing into a perpetual mist. It has been reported that each night, a mysterious fog rolls over the Chickamauga battlefield, a phenomenon that is absent outside park grounds.

Witnesses swear that this tiger's eyes burn bright at night while the animal stalks the battlefield.

Yet another legend of Old Green Eyes comes from a battlefield monument dedicated to the 125th Ohio Infantry. The men fought so bravely at Snodgrass Hill that their divisional commander, Thomas Wood, named them the Tiger Regiment, and they were called "Opdycke's Tigers" for their commander, Colonel Emerson Opdycke. The 125th Ohio lost seventeen killed, eighty-three wounded and five missing at Snodgrass Hill.

Atop the monument is a prowling stone tiger carved from stone. The green eyes are said to belong to the wild animal that patrols the hill at night, seeking the regiment's casualties, its emerald eyes glowing menacingly at visitors.

Kaczmarek felt "very queer at Snodgrass Hill…I did not spend a lot of time on the hill because of this overpowering feeling."

Ghost Horses

Two friends, Kriss and Mark, took a short vacation to Chickamauga on the anniversary of the battle. Although they found the woods, fields and trails of the battlefield rainy, foggy and dark, the men decided to explore an area near Snodgrass Hill. On a trail through the forest, "we heard a loud stomping noise," they informed the website ghoststudies.com, "like a big horse stomping on dry earth," although the ground was saturated with rain. They continued the exploration and "heard the stomping noise again, and a snort. Really loud, and very close." Before quitting for the night, they heard artillery and rifle fire.

Band Practice

Doug Albritton is a scoutmaster in north Georgia who takes Cub Scouts and Boy Scouts camping on the Chickamauga battlefield. In order to tire them out one summer evening, he organized a game of capture the flag, dividing the youths into teams and planting a flag and lantern at the top of Snodgrass Hill. The defenders soon heard the sounds of drums and flutes atop the elevation, according to Georgiana C. Kotarski in *Ghosts of the Southern Tennessee Valley*. Fearing that a trick was being played, a Scout reported the phenomenon to Albritton. He sent the younger boys to camp and ascended the hill with the older lads. They heard "Civil War–type music" near the cabin. At the log structure, the music ceased, and he heard the sound of a dozen people running for the woods.

The eleven members of the Snodgrass family were home when fighting broke out during the war, but as their home was transformed into a Federal field hospital, they fled for a wooded ravine. There they listened to the roar of battle, the silence of victory and, finally, a Confederate band that played joyfully. Perhaps those were the sounds heard that late summer evening.

Kotarski told of John Hodges, who was cruising the park in 1964, searching for Green Eyes with a Ford convertible full of fellow high school seniors. Parking near the Wilder Tower, they walked into a field, where a light abruptly winked into existence. The light, six feet off the ground and bluish-green, approached through trees and underbrush and split into two lights at a distance of one hundred yards. At that point, the boys conceded the field, leaping into the car and racing away to a loud sound like a shot. The noise turned out to be a rod that cracked beneath the car. Only extreme heat could have caused it, a mechanic believed. John's brother, Jim, a witness and later a tackle at Memphis State University, said, "It scared the pee out of me."

On the night of October 20, 2001, four members of the Foundation for Paranormal Research (FPR) visited Chickamauga to search for Old

Green Eyes at Snodgrass Hill. Jennifer McElhannon wrote that the team, including Olivia Newton and Terry Dimbrell, "felt surrounded and sad" with emotions, "enough to fill your mind for a lifetime."

They interviewed a ranger who had been patrolling the park after closing hours one night and received reports of trespassers. Investigating, he drove to the area and found two adults and two children running at full speed. He stopped the family and found them in a hysterical state. While walking through a field, they suddenly became alarmed for no discernible reason and then experienced what they thought was a scent of alcohol. The four looked around and saw nothing but decided to exit the area rapidly. As they ran, an arm appeared from nowhere and scratched one of the adults. The ranger confirmed that the man's shirt was torn, and several scratches were still bleeding. When the ranger searched the area where the incident had occurred, he found nothing visible, but he did experience a horrible stench that could not have emanated from a drunken vagrant.

The ranger pointed out the Opdycke-Tiger monument as the place haunted by Old Green Eyes. The team took many photos and was rewarded with a number of mists and orbs captured by different cameras. Orbs bounced around in different directions, including a small one that shot rapidly across large areas. A golden orb was photographed around the Opdycke-Tiger monument, and a separate frame showed a mist surrounding it.

The Lady in White

Another denizen of Snodgrass Hill is a woman dressed all in white. Many say that her beautiful attire is the wedding gown that she never got to wear in life because her fiancé was killed on this wilderness battlefield. She was buried in the gown and floats across the battlefield night after night, torch held high, searching the fields and woods for him, most often in September and October, but she disappears if witnesses get too close. On the night after the last day of battle, women searched the field for the bodies of loved ones, their lantern lights bobbing erratically as their cries of despair mingled with the screams and moans of the wounded. The lights and cries are still detected by some. Another version has a woman in a white dress singing lullabies to an infant cradled in her arms. That vision is usually observed at dusk and during reenactments of the battle, which occur off-site due to National Park Service rules.

The soldier in the only marked grave at Chickamauga is thought to prowl the battlefield while his fiancée searches for him in her wedding dress.

One popular story postulates that a local woman, Abigail Reed (a bridge on the battlefield is named for her family), was engaged to John Ingraham, who joined the Confederate army and served in the First Georgia. After the battle, she found him dead on the battlefield, where he was buried. Probably the only true part of the story is Ingraham's grave on Alexander Bridge Road, the only marked grave on the battlefield. Ingraham, killed late on September 19, was buried by two friends, Charles and James Reed, on their family's property near where the private died.

John Fogarty described a woman who regularly visits Ingraham's grave and purports to converse with his spirit, "which hovers about, soaking up the attention." Fogarty's girlfriend was "seriously creeped out" near the Poe Cabin in the summer of 2000, when she noticed "someone moving through the grass behind her, [she] whirled around to see who it was, and actually *saw* the grass being stepped on, as if some unseen human was walking toward her. She said, 'Are you friend or foe?' and the thing turned away from her and paced into the woods."

The Power of the Tower

Many ghost stories at Chickamauga center on the eighty-five-foot-high stone observation platform called the Wilder Tower, constructed in 1903 by veterans of Colonel John T. Wilder's brigade. Many men died here at the battle, and during the Spanish-American War, a U.S. Army training camp was located on a hill behind the tower, where more soldiers died of typhoid

This riderless horse statue at Chickamauga is symbolic of war's cost, as well as of the spirit animals occasionally heard and seen racing across the battlefield.

fever and other diseases. Ranger Jeffery Leathers told Dale Kaczmarek that the structure's cornerstone originally contained a number of souvenirs. When the cornerstone was opened during bicentennial events in 1976, it was found to be empty, despite showing no evidence that it had been previously disturbed. The artifacts had simply vanished.

Ranger Charlie Fisher said that in about 1970, several youths were prowling around the Wilder Tower in the dark. One climbed a lightning rod fourteen feet up, squirmed through an observation slit and then continued up the stairs to the top. He yelled to his friends below, who were drinking beer. A few moments later, the friends heard a scream of terror, and the daredevil leaped through another slit and fell twenty-five feet to the cement below. He was permanently paralyzed and has never revealed what had so frightened him. However, *Blue & Gray* magazine claimed that he was spooked by noises originating from the buddies throwing empty beer cans against the metal door at ground level.

Another tower story has a young mother dropping her infant from the top and then instantly jumping after it. Photos taken around the tower often manifest unexplainable abnormalities.

You Can Stay Forever

The Census of the Dead website hosted several submitted Chickamauga stories. One was from a woman who had attended a religious college in the area during the mid-1980s and frequently visited the battlefield with her fiancé and other friends. On several occasions, they heard "groaning or crying coming from the woods" near the Minnesota monument. One day, a group of seven students (six girls and a boy) approached the area and were alarmed to find a dozen bikers drinking at the memorial. They were considering a tactical withdrawal when "this blood curdling scream came from behind the monument," the woman recorded. "The bikers hi-tailed it out of there," but the students decided to check out the phantom screamer. They heard "heavy breathing" but failed to find a material source of the audio and decamped.

On another occasion, in the month of November, three couples were fooling around at the top of the Wilder monument. Two couples left, leaving Sarah and David. They soon followed, but halfway down, David remembered that he had left his coat and trotted up to collect it. At the top, the future meteorologist stopped to watch the clouds, until he heard a woman's voice say, "Are you coming or not?" He assumed it was Sarah, but she was sitting in the car with the other two women, while the men stood beside it staring up at David.

"Just a minute, I'm coming," David replied.

"Take your time," the voice calmly stated. "You can stay forever if you want." David, taking that to mean that Sarah was angry, hurried down to the car, disturbed at not finding his girlfriend on the stairs.

"As we were leaving," the woman wrote, "one of the guys pointed to the tower and we all looked to see a woman on top."

The Phantom Tower

The six students hastened from the scene but decided to cruise the battlefield to "calm ourselves down." They ended up on a gravel service road so narrow that they could not turn around and were surprised to find that the road ended at a second tower, similar to the Wilder structure. The surrounding grounds were overgrown. They ignored the "No Trespassing" sign and found the door to the tower sealed by cement blocks. The students had heard that Satanists sought out isolated areas of the park for their ceremonies, and as evidence, they located a spray-painted pentagram on the side of the tower and numerous places where fires had burned.

"Then we heard this really weird sound, like someone knocking on a door—a wooden door, but there wasn't anything like that anywhere around there," the woman wrote. That was followed by a "low moaning sound that rose, crescendoed and then faded away."

That incident motivated the students to jump into their car and speed away. They related their story to a park ranger, who lectured them about visiting the site. Although she searched repeatedly for the second tower, "I could never find it again." Probably it never existed, at least in this realm. It certainly is not extant today.

B. Keith Toney is an accomplished historian, author and battlefield guide. In his book *Battlefield Ghosts*, he admitted that he has no personal ghost stories to relate, but an incident while traveling as a boy with his father left a deep impression on him. "I had the bejezus scared out of me one memorable day when I was about 10 years old," he noted. "My father and I were touring the battlefield…when an uneasy feeling stopped me dead in my tracks. I went back to the car while my dad continued on by himself. At least I think he was by himself."

The Knight Who Says "Amy"

In 1990, Linda Gilstrap, a Fort Oglethorpe resident, was sixteen and enjoying a hayride through the park with ten friends. While stopped at the Wilder Tower, they spotted a flaming torch in a nearby field. It repeatedly appeared, disappeared and appeared again. The group was further startled by the sound of horse hooves rapidly approaching, followed by the arrival of a spirit horse sporting green eyes and ridden by a skeleton clad in a Confederate uniform. The specter dismounted and said "Amy" repeatedly before it vanished.

Ghost Rider

At Shiloh, Confederate brigadier general William B. Bate nearly lost a leg, shattered by a bullet. The general drew his pistol and threatened to shoot the surgeons who wanted to amputate—he kept the leg but used a crutch for the rest of his life. At Chickamauga, Bate led his brigade in an attack so fierce that three horses were killed under him. The sight of the dead mounts so impressed President Jefferson Davis that he promoted Bate to major general. It might be the ghost of Bate, or another Confederate officer, that is seen on the battlefield today, riding a spectral horse. According to Debra Glass and Heath Mathews in *Skeletons of the Civil War*, Russ, a local resident from Fort Oglethorpe, was traveling through the battlefield following a late shift at a restaurant when a mounted ghost soldier waving a sword appeared in the illumination from his headlights. Russ sped off, believing that he had seen a spectral officer and horse of the Civil War.

Old Green Eyes at the Wilder Tower

Denise Smith is another citizen of Fort Oglethorpe. In 1980, she left her job at a restaurant and drove home through the park. "It was raining and foggy, so I was going real slow," she said. "I was going through the S-curve past Wilder Tower when I saw something big in the road about eye level, and all I could see were these big green eyes. It was so foggy I couldn't see a body. I got closer, and it just disappeared." For the past quarter of a century, Denise has refused to enter the park after dark.

The great-great-grandparents of Irene Staub, John and Eliza Glenn, lived on land occupied by the haunted Wilder Tower. John was serving in the Confederate army when Union general Rosecrans used their home as his headquarters. "I do know that not too far from the tower, accidents have happened in the same spot where [they] lived," Irene declared. "When the rangers take accident reports, they see eyes glowing in the night."

Guardian Angel

An anonymous posting to the website Ghosts Along the Southern Road described an experience atop the Wilder Tower when the witness was four or five. He and his grandfather had climbed the monument, and he "was looking out the turrets on top and leaned over to see the base of the tower." The lad leaned so far that he might have fallen to his death. However, "I felt a hand on my shoulder pull me back." Thinking it had been his grandfather, the youth turned and found the man on the other side of the tower, staring intently into the distance. No one else was present.

The Tower Claims Another Life

On July 4, 2004, the Wilder Tower witnessed another mysterious death, that of Crystal Housley, a thirty-six-year-old single mother who lived in nearby Rossville. At 9:15 p.m., park ranger Eduardo Cartaya was making his rounds of the park and had just arrived to lock up the tower. Approaching the hilltop structure, he spotted Housley standing on the crown, the tallest part of the monument. Cartaya talked to the woman and thought that he had convinced her to climb off the crown and meet him at the base of the monument. Seeing the lady heading back for the observation platform, Cartaya started for the ground-floor entrance. Apparently, Housley immediately climbed back onto the crown and threw herself off. Cartaya did not see the fall, but he heard the body impact the ground twenty-five feet from the foot of the monument. The ranger locked the tower in case someone had been with the woman and found her body. Although Housley was having domestic problems, she had just started a new job and purchased a car. She "seemed happier than she had been for a long time," said a relative. The Walker County coroner ruled the death a suicide.

Rumor has it that this is the third death at the tower since 1903.

Déjà Vu All Over Again

In *Echoes of Valor*, Nannette Morrison related the following tale. Willis Francis Marion Edwards fought first in the Eighth Georgia Cavalry and then became part of Company H, Eighth Georgia Infantry, until his death at Chickamauga. His great-grandson is Bill Edwards, a reenactor, and in 1988, on the 125th anniversary of the great battle, Bill Edwards, his son and two friends left the reenactment site for the twelve-mile trip to the actual battlefield. It was late, and a heavy mist was turning into rain as the sky darkened. The men were searching for a small monument that marked the place where the Eighth Georgia had fought and where Bill's ancestor had died. They had looked for some time and were about to abandon the effort when Bill felt a strong psychic message to "turn here!" Edwards veered onto a narrow gravel road that descended a hill. They approached the rear of a small marker and stopped. Bill and his son, Mike, walked to the front of the monument, with Bill experiencing cold chills unrelated to the weather. The memorial indicated that Company H, Eighth Georgia, had stood and fought here, where Willis F.M. Edwards had given the last full measure of devotion.

Georgiana C. Kotarski described Jimmy Haun, a farmer who had a government contract to gather the hay grown in the extensive fields on the Chickamauga battlefield. On a number of occasions, he was harvesting near Lytle Field and Dyer House when he observed a Confederate soldier leaning against a cannon representing Dent's Alabama Battery. The man wore high boots, and his face was shaded by a slouch hat. "I drove right by him," Haun stated. "But he never acknowledged me. I waved at him, and he never waved back. He just stood there."

When the hay was ripe for harvest, Haun labored until the job was done, hoping that rain would not fall. Working at night on the battlefield unnerved him. He often heard strange sounds and saw unusual flashing lights, but that is not what frightened him. Haun used an old dump truck, and in front of Lytle Field, his headlights would "just go off right there." He would make a run every hour and a half, and it happened every time. Nights in the park are dark, and Haun would slowly creep out, his head out the window. "[O]nce I got outside the park they'd come back on." Of course, nothing was found wrong with the electrical system. "My wife won't go in there at night by herself," Haun said. "She don't feel safe in there at night."

Haun stopped working at Chickamauga after the sun went down. "Go out at midnight and stand around for about fifteen minutes," he explained. "You'll leave with a respect for the place, I promise you that."

In her book *Miracles from Heaven*, Barbara Duffy described a woman named Julia who has been "sensitive to the supernatural" her entire life. At historic places, "spirits appear before her." As she exited the museum at Chickamauga, "she saw the silent images of the Confederate army pass before her." She saw artillery pulled by horses, mounted officers mouthing silent commands and marching soldiers. The moment passed, and she was back in the present. When she described the incident to a park ranger, he admitted that "quite a few people had seen similar activity in that same spot over the years."

The Story of a Man and His Dog

On October 29, 1997, a man who posts online with the name "AoT" put his faithful companion, Frank, a one-hundred-pound Tennessee coon dog, in his pickup truck and drove to Chickamauga. They spent the night in a family hotel and hit the battlefield trails at first light. Frank has explored many battlefields with AoT and rarely strays more than two hundred yards from him. When Frank does run off, he always meets his owner at the truck.

As dusk fell, AoT was searching for a monument in Vinnard Field. After locating the marker, he started calling for Frank. The park was pitch black by 8:00 p.m., with no moon, as AoT walked to his truck and continued calling. After ten minutes, he decided to leave a message at the visitors' center so he could be contacted when Frank showed up.

AoT drove slowly toward Chickamauga Creek, stopping every two hundred yards to shout for the dog and listen for a reply. At Winfrey Field, he heard someone else call, "Frank. Frank"—not loudly, and about three hundred yards into the woods. He waited thirty seconds and called for the dog again, and again he heard the voice, "Frank. Frank."

AoT grabbed a flashlight and started into the deep woods. As he marched a quarter mile into the forest, "I can hear something in the woods, like a deer, clearly moving through the brush," he related. "It keeps moving away from me and someone calling 'Frank. Frank,'" was several hundred yards to his front.

When AoT entered a one-hundred-yard wide clearing, he said, "I Know I saw something on the other side of the small field in the tree line," he wrote. "It was dressed in white, like a white or tan colored duster [coat]. I stood there for a moment, called, 'Here Frank.'" He studied the stationary figure but was distracted by the sudden baying of Frank. Looking back, he found that the figure "Was Not There."

Frank bayed while he was following a trail but barked when he had treed a raccoon. Frank was baying, but the sound seemed to remain in the same place, about two miles to the north. Between the baying, he heard the same voice, "Frank. Frank," also moving north. "I made tracks!" AoT wrote.

As AoT retraced his route, he stopped to listen for Frank. "Every time I stop to listen, I know there is something in the brush Following Me, stopping each time I do, but not in time to completely avoid me hearing it." At the truck, AoT concluded that Frank was badly hurt. "He was not baying with his usual excitement, there is an element of hurt in it." He feared that Frank had encountered an animal trap. After two-thirds of a mile, AoT abandoned the truck because no roads led toward Frank's position.

"And damnit if it does not start again, between my calls someone off to the right is calling out, 'Frank.' Not calling out loud, more like just saying it."

AoT climbed a hill and found Frank, who was "on his belly at the foot of a monument howling to beat the band. I am shocked, no coon in sight, nothing treed and at least 4 miles away from where we were when he and I had gotten separated. There is nothing there, he is just baying for no good reason at all. He is not on the feet and not hurt. The dog literally leaps onto my chest…he was scared to death…He is shivering and even as I am trying to calm him down he keeps baying at the top of his lungs. Finally I have to sit down next to him and put my arms around him to calm him down." It took ten minutes for Frank to subside, but soon after, the dog relaxed and laid his head in AoT's lap.

Suddenly, Frank "jumps up to his feet like a shot and for only the second time in his life I heard old Frank growl. Well that was more than enough for me, I cannot make anything out, it is as dark as the bottom of a well. I make a command decision. We are getting the HELL out of there."

Man and dog raced down the hill. Frank arrived first and "jumped into the bed and busted the back window to the cab crawling in. I kid you not if that dog had the keys with him he would have been a half mile down the road by the time I got there! We drove like bats out of hell." The dog did not sleep one second that night.

AoT returned to the park the following morning and discovered the memorial where Frank was baying was the Tennessee monument. At the visitors' center, a ranger confirmed that many people had complained of an animal howling during the night. However, the sounds were heard until 3:00 a.m., and AoT and Frank had decamped by 10:30 p.m.

Sadness at the Kelly House

A woman posting at the website The Shadowlands with the Internet name "msdixiebelle36" drove through Chickamauga and made a report to the Shadowlands website. She often allows her "senses" to "pick up something out of the ordinary," and on this occasion, she felt led to stop at the Kelly House. After observing it for several minutes, she "felt drawn" to it. She approached the structure with trepidation, finding the door padlocked. "Still I put my hand against the door and the anger I felt being emitted from that house almost knocked me to my knees," she revealed. "The sadness surrounding it was almost tangible and I could feel tears welling up in my eyes. But what truly sat me back on my heels was the sound of crying coming from within that building. It was a deep, mournful, soul wrenching cry." She circled the house. "All the way around this building I could hear this wailing from inside. The sadness was so intense that I had to leave." She was surprised that other visitors did not hear the crying.

Various cabins on the Chickamauga battlefield, used as hospitals, elicit feelings of grief and suffering, and weeping is heard from their interiors.

On Bloody Pond

On the night of January 1, 2005, Internet poster "SuzyQnTN" and her sister journeyed to the Bloody Pond, found off parkland on a residential street near railroad tracks. Now a field, during the battle, wounded soldiers struggled here for water, tinting it red with their blood. The photos the women took revealed large orbs, a blood-red energy ribbon and a white energy rod on the same picture. The temperature dropped steadily during their visit, and after ignoring a "very odd feeling, kind of 'electrified,' and a 'get out of there or something is going to happen that you don't want to happen!'" sense for a while, they drove home.

The Deer Hunters and Other Stories

In October 1996, Internet poster "Carolineblue823," a retired chemist, visited Chickamauga with her husband and children. Writing on the Moonlit Road Message Board, she said that she "was somewhat annoyed at the sound of gunshots that disturbed the otherwise peaceful park."

She thought that the shots originated with deer hunters, only later realizing that there was no hunting allowed in the park. At Longstreet's breakthrough field, her "attention was caught by movement in the tree line…lots of it," which she attributed to the passage of deer, although she also "wondered what was reflecting light in brief flashes on the deer." Perhaps Bambi and company were packing bayoneted rifles for defense.

On Snodgrass Hill, "I felt a most unusual sadness and depression" on that beautiful fall day, "culminating in an uncharacteristic crying fit which I couldn't explain, nor could I stop." Comparing notes with the family, none had heard, seen or felt anything out of the ordinary. Caroline probably has undiscovered psychic abilities.

Reenactors have had several eerie experiences at Chickamauga. One man dressed as a Federal soldier for a living history demonstration was strolling along a roadway at dusk when a Confederate soldier suddenly appeared. The Yank smiled and stopped to chat with his fellow reenactor, but the Rebel leveled his rifle and took aim. Forgetting that he was shooting blanks, the reenactor quickly brought up his weapon, but the Confederate instantly vanished. The man later refused to enter that area of the park except in bright sunshine.

In 1998, David Lester and other reenactors established a camp to enable visitors to understand Civil War life during Living History Days. Noting a neighboring camp, they wandered over and talked with their comrades for several hours. In the morning, the reenactors returned to find no trace of a camp—there were no campfire remains or any other signs that anyone had been there recently.

In the late 1980s, a group of living history demonstrators walking along a road in the Environmental Study Area at night reported being trailed by a strange orange light. Identical incidents have occurred at other battlefields.

The Adventures of Scott and Kat

On the Northwest Georgia Paranormal Investigation Team's (NGPI) message board on October 23, 2005, Scott wrote that on numerous trips to Chickamauga, "I have experienced a lot of noises and things moving around in the woods," and he found the Alabama and Georgia monuments "especially active." That night, he and Kat headed for Chickamauga again. After parking, they "heard what sounded like a person whistling." They pursued the source of the sound and found it changed—it now "sounded like a pig squealing," and the location of the noise had also shifted. As they closed in on it a second time, "the sound changed yet again," this time to a bird. When they drove off, the sound emanated from "both sides of the road." This sound phenomenon is a frequent occurrence at paranormal events.

The route to Snodgrass Hill was closed, so they attempted to find it on a dirt road. At an intersection, Scott wrote,

> *I saw something i never thought i would see.* Old Green Eyes. *Kat and i both saw two extremely bright green eyes in a tree about 10 feet off the ground. I didnt even take time to think, i grabbed up my spotlight and ran as fast as i could to the edge of the road. About 50 feet into the woods, there he was. I saw 2 bright glowing green eyes bobbing up and down thru the woods as if it were something walking. The eyes were about 4 feet off the ground, probably 3 inches in diameter, and it made no sound. You would think if it were some kind of creature, it would be making noise. I observed the eyes for maybe 5 seconds until it just vanished. The underbrush was so thick i couldnt see anything but the eyes.*

Exhilarated, they continued on to the Wilder Tower, where they heard "a loud pop sound that seemed to come from within the tower." The night's experience convinced Scott that Green Eyes was real.

The NGPI Team has naturally investigated Chickamauga a number of times and always encounters anomalies, particularly EMF readings. Simply walking down a lane on the battlefield, suddenly "you'll have electromagnetic energy spikes" and "temperature fluctuation" of thirty degrees, followed by a return to normal within seconds, and you "can hear twigs snapping around you." Members also report feelings of being watched. One night, half a dozen investigators felt like "somebody's staring at you." Photographically, they have captured a "foggy apparition," and at a one-lane bridge across Chickamauga Creek, a picture "has so many orbs that you can't count them."

More Ghost Busters

"I believe that it is a possibility that Confederate soldiers still roam the Chickamauga battlefield," said Mike Watkins—a LaFayette resident, law enforcement officer and member of the NGPI—to Katie Ward of the *Walker County Messenger* in 2004. "There were 34,000 casualties during the battle of Chickamauga," he added. The electromagnetic anomalies are particularly interesting because the battlefield has no electricity.

At about 6:30 p.m. in December 2003, message board poster "nightsky," her husband and their two children arrived by car to roam the battlefield roads in search of wildlife. They found nothing and had stopped to turn around when one "heard a moan that got louder and louder like someone was in agony." All were frightened by the experience, the husband so badly that he got lost. Three months later, she returned to Chickamauga and captured the image of a man on horseback on her camcorder.

Rich Kanan is a Michigan Yankee with a Rebel ancestor who fought at Chickamauga: Lieutenant Newton Jasper Smiley, Company G, Thirty-second Tennessee Infantry. For a number of years, Kanan has portrayed a soldier with the Twelfth South Carolina and the Fourth Michigan "for some fun and history all rolled into one," he explained.

On the anniversary of Chickamauga, Kanan and his family were visiting the battlefield, he in Union uniform. He posed for a picture near Widow Glenn Field, and no anomalies appeared until the film was developed. In the background is the image of a horse without rider, the figure of a uniformed soldier and faces in the trees. The family did not remember seeing any horses in the park on that occasion, although research proved that several cavalry units had been present there in September 1863.

"The whole time I was at the Chickamauga National Battlefield Park I had a strange sense of being watched," Kanan wrote. "I felt like someone was staring at me, watching my every move." As he posed, "I do remember having a calm sense of peace and then the feeling of many eyes on me, but I knew no one was around." He found the sensation "seriously disturbing."

Other visitors to Chickamauga report hearing phantom footsteps running through the wilderness and an unfelt wind that ruffles bushes. Unseen men are heard crying, moaning and mumbling, and there are reports of muffled gunshots. A local minister confided anonymously to a ranger that he had seen a horseman ride swiftly past—with no head.

On the night of January 24, 2009, teams from Ghost Hunters of Southern Tennessee (GHOST) investigated Chickamauga. Three of the four teams involved sighted "a full body apparition at the end of the row of cannons next to the Snodgrass cabin," noted their website. Also, two teams spotted "a floating green light." One team pursued "but was unable to keep up through the brush and trees."

Some years ago, I was teaching the Civil War to one of my U.S. history classes. After describing the carnage that had occurred near Chickamauga Creek, I revealed that the Cherokee word meant "river of death." One of my students, Jordan, gasped and exclaimed, "I live on the river of death?" Her home sits on Chickamauga Street, although far from the battlefield.

Chickamauga stories continue to evolve. It is reported that a ghoulish monster lurks beneath the staircase of the Wilder Tower at night, and the top four stairs are said to have bloodstains. The marks have been scrubbed away many times, people claim, but they always return. The pervasive nighttime fog has sometimes been reported as being green.

The River of Death still flows. Murders and suicides continue to occur in the park, and big-city criminals dump bodies in the woods. Be careful after dark, both of the living and of the dead.

Village of Chickamauga

In addition to the thoroughly haunted Chickamauga battlefield is the nearby village of Chickamauga, which is also a hotbed of paranormal activity. In 1863, this was a small community centered on Crawfish Springs, a significant water source, and the Gordon-Lee Mansion. During and following the battle, the village was inundated with wounded and dying Confederate and Federal soldiers, and the house was a major hospital center. The mansion, said to be haunted by some of the men who died there, is available for weddings, receptions, luncheons and other events and is open for tours.

Joan Jackson and her family moved into their new home on Cleburne Street in July 1967. A year later, "I had carpet put in the kitchen," Joan said, "and I came in one day and saw green ink poured on it. We could not find the ink. Then, I came in and saw buttermilk thrown on the kitchen cabinets." Soon afterward, Joan and other family members saw figures in the corners of their eyes. More startling events followed. "I saw two Confederate soldiers, dirty, standing in my yard by my flower bed," Joan related, "and thirty minutes later, a lady walked across my driveway. She was in a long denim dress in a bonnet with a basket." On another occasion, Joan was in the basement when she heard footsteps above her that started descending the stairs. She bravely swatted at the air above the sounds but detected nothing.

Joan brought in a psychic, who identified the soldiers as Ed and Joe. They indicated their unhappiness over the new house but did like a pond she constructed on the property. Joan last saw the men during the summer of 2004.

Another haunted site in Chickamauga is a place with an awful name, Longstreet's Charge Condominiums, adjacent to Crawfish Springs, an important hospital site. When the structure was a restaurant, said Joan Jackson, the ghost of a Civil War nurse would materialize and drive off the waitresses.

Margaret, her husband and their elementary school–age granddaughter live in a house off Cloud Springs Road in Fort Oglethorpe. Margaret explained that they might not be the only residents: "I can't say I believe in ghosts, but something strange is going on."

The first act of strangeness occurred one night while she relaxed in her recliner. Just inside a bedroom doorway appeared a Confederate soldier. "He had his face to the wall," she told Kevin Cumming of the *Walker County Messenger*, "and in the blink of an eye, he was gone."

Months later, another man, this one not a soldier, assumed the same position. Then, unusual gray mists, three to four feet in height, suddenly materialized within the house and then dissipated just as quickly. Several months after that, the Confederate warrior reappeared, this time in the backyard, taking his leisure in a lawn chair. Margaret was angry, not frightened, when the phantom whacked her in the back of the head while she occupied her recliner.

There was only one more paranormal incident that occurred in the house, but it gave Margaret a fright. One night, she awoke to answer the call of nature. Several feet from the bed, she saw a small girl standing in a flowing nightgown. Naturally assuming that it was her granddaughter, Margaret reached for her, but the figure disappeared. The granddaughter was found sound asleep in bed, wearing pajamas and not a gown. "That is the only thing that has scared me," she admitted.

Lafayette

The Haunted High School

Nearby Lafayette is the location of the stately Gordon Lee High School, a beautiful brick structure with grand white columns and old willows and oaks shading the lawn. Although the school was constructed in 1932, I am certain that disembodied spirits from Chickamauga could mistake it for their era and seek refuge within. Students and visitors alike have experienced feelings of foreboding and loss, and the sounds of ghostly conversations, laughter and marching have been heard reverberating through the halls. A portrait of one of the institution's namesakes, Robert E. Lee, is occasionally seen staring at people.

According to Leslie Rule, author of *Coast to Coast Ghosts*, in the mid-1990s, Greg Greenhaw was a social studies teacher and coach at Gordon Lee. "The school is haunted," he flatly declared, and he had an "eerie feeling" at night. When patrolling police officers found doors unlocked or lights on after dark, they called Greenhaw to accompany them as a matter of "protocol." Greenhaw thought that there was another reason. "You guys are afraid of ghosts," he teased them. One older officer frankly agreed. "He told me he heard laughter and voices when the school was empty," Greenhaw said, and the man also heard the phantom footsteps.

Rome

Rome was a major Confederate manufacturing and hospital center, and General Sherman occupied the city in May 1864 after a brief Confederate rear guard action. Rome's charming Myrtle Hill Cemetery towers above the scenic city and its surrounding countryside. Near the entrance at ground level is a section containing the remains of four hundred Confederates who died in local hospitals. Figures of ghostly soldiers have been sighted in the area, and high atop the hill, where a monument to the "Lost Cause" stands, mysterious hovering lights and the ghost of a lady are seen.

CAVE SPRINGS

To the southwest of Chickamauga is the charming village of Cave Springs, where several old buildings from the former Georgia School for the Deaf remain preserved. In 1846, the O.P. Fannin School for the Deaf was opened by Fannin in a one-room log cabin with four students. When Fannin Hall opened two years later, there were fourteen pupils. The school closed from 1861 to 1865 for the war, when the structure was used as a hospital. Within Fannin Hall, blood still stains floors and walls, and the sounds of crying and phantom footsteps are heard. Legend has it that a psychic, employed to investigate the building, blanched at the entrance and said that the structure housed too many evil spirits to allow entrance. Another report claimed that deer feeding in the field surrounding the complex are seen to flee just before the appearance of a female ghost that wanders across the land.

On January 12, 2008, a team from GHOST conducted an investigation at Fannin Hall. "While setting up the equipment," its website related, "one man had his necklace mysteriously broken from his neck," leaving marks on the skin. During the night, members of different teams experienced similar phenomena in the same locations, including "having their hair pulled, sighting 'shadow people,' being touched, hearing noises/voices and getting physically ill." Adult male and children's voices were recorded, including one child saying "Stop…Mark." Unexplainable shadows, lights, mists and apparitions were detected on photographs. One shadow figure was captured down a hall where investigators heard footsteps.

PART II
SPIRITS OF THE ATLANTA CAMPAIGN

After Chickamauga, the besieged Union army in Chattanooga was massively reinforced by Ulysses S. Grant and William T. Sherman and their Army of the Tennessee. In November, twin Union victories at Lookout Mountain and Missionary Ridge routed Confederate forces. Grant left to fight Robert E. Lee in Virginia, and in May 1864, Sherman set out for Atlanta with an army of 120,000 Federals. Opposing him was Joseph E. Johnston's 60,000 Confederates. The armies would advance and retreat, probe and parry, flank and fight until Atlanta was captured in early September. The route of their campaign was littered with death and ruin. Today, many spirits continue the struggle.

RINGGOLD

After Grant crushed Bragg's army in Chattanooga, the Union pursuit was stopped at Ringgold Gap by the gallantry of Confederate general Patrick Cleburne's men. The "Great Locomotive Chase" ended nearby, and the area was a no-man's-land between November 1863 and May 1864. A Union captain died on the grounds of Boynton (1918), where an officer's uniform buttons have been excavated. His ghost haunts the front room, making rapping and banging noises around people he does not like and performing parlor tricks for nice folks. His full figure appears at bedside, where he has been known to crawl under the covers with the living. Local legend claims that he is awaiting a letter from his sister somewhere in Yankeedom.

In the summer of 1945, Don Howell was nearly five when his family attended a family function in Ringgold. They met in the antebellum home of an aunt and uncle, a structure that had been used as a hospital following the Battle of Chickamauga. Howell heard his elders speak of the "haunted house" and asked an older cousin, Jerry, what they meant.

"We have ghosts upstairs," he replied. Jerry then led a procession of cousins to "the room," which contained nothing—no furniture, no storage; it was simply bare. Jerry explained that "this room was where they brought soldiers to die," Howell wrote in a column for the *Cordele Dispatch* on November 18, 2008.

All gawked at the "dark bloodstains on the wood floors and initials and dates carved into the walls." When the other children left, Howell remained, his gaze transfixed on a wall. As he looked, "images began to appear. Suddenly men who appeared old and tired filled the room. Some were lying on thin narrow mattresses with no sheets." One man lay on a bed without pillow or sheet.

"As I stood watching the scene unfold the man on the bed pushed himself up on one elbow and seemed to look straight at me. He didn't speak but I still can feel his hopelessness." The soldiers wore "tattered pants and torn shirts." Some had only pants; others long underwear. Some were gaunt, hollow-cheeked or toothless.

"What stands out though is the look on the face of each man. There was a pervasive sadness and loneliness. Even then I knew they wanted to go home but were resigned to never again seeing the face of a loved one. The sense of despair and helplessness was palpable, even to a four-year-old boy."

Howell has wondered if he saw a psychic flashback or had stepped into a time warp. He has wondered if perhaps it had been manufactured by his imagination, "but if concocted, from what was it constructed?" Half a century later, he still wonders. Unfortunately, the house was torn down years ago.

The Old Stone Church

Just south of Ringgold on U.S. 41 is the Old Stone Church, constructed in 1850. Its sixteen-inch-thick sandstone walls were quarried locally, and

Bloodstains inside the Old Stone Church near Ringgold mark the building as a Civil War hospital. Psychic phenomena are common at that spot.

the beams were hand-hewn. The original pews remain. After the battles at Missionary Ridge and Ringgold, the building was used as a hospital.

On one trip to northern Georgia five years ago, we were delighted to find the Old Stone Church open and staffed. I photographed the bloodstains on the ancient wooden floor near the front doors to the church and approached the volunteer at the back of the building. I introduced myself and told him that I was on a ghostly mission.

The man smiled and said, "I saw you taking pictures of the bloodstains. We have had a few ghost hunters in the building, and that is the place where they have photographed odd things, and that is where they got some ghostly taped sayings and where members say they 'feel' things."

"Now, I don't put much trust in those things," he continued, "but I will tell you something that happened to me several times. Sometimes, when I am sitting here reading, that door down there by the bloodstains will swing open for no reason. I always get up and look outside, but there are never any people around and the wind wasn't blowing. That door does not open easily. But that's what I've personally experienced. It's made me think."

Tunnel Hill

Georgia's first railroad tunnel pierced Chetoogeta Ridge just north of Dalton. As Sherman's first objective, a number of skirmishes were fought here, and large units of soldiers camped in the area, their sick and wounded cared for in local hospitals. Cleburne's division was stationed here during the winter of 1863–64, where shelter, clothing and food were short as they awaited the Union advance. Reenactments and encampments are held on the land surrounding Meadowbrook, an antebellum home located near the tunnel.

Connie Scott, who writes feature stories for the Dalton newspaper, lives in Tunnel Hill with her family and has extensively researched Civil War ghosts in her hometown. Most of the stories originated with Ken Sumner, a preservationist and reenactor captain with the Thirty-fifth Tennessee Infantry Reenactment Group from Woodstock who became interested in the tunnel before it was restored.

Sumner once told people that the Tunnel Hill battlefield was not haunted, but he has changed his tune, saying, "The field is definitely haunted. Peculiar experiences began happening to me in 1993 and have continued since that time with varying degrees of intensity."

One foggy morning, as Sumner approached the tunnel with a group, they observed a figure forming in the mist. As they walked closer, "it became obvious that the shape was a sharp, distinct outline of a human standing just inside the tunnel mouth," Sumner recalled. The figure disappeared as they neared. Sumner thought that it was the ghost of a Civil War soldier. Since renovation, people in the tunnel have heard screams, seen soldiers and been pushed or just touched by phantoms.

Sumner related one unique tunnel story to Corrina Underwood in *Haunted History: Atlanta and North Georgia*. While taking a group through the tube, a train was approaching the other end. For a moment, it seemed as though the locomotive had bypassed the modern, adjacent tunnel and was thundering toward them, its headlight illuminating the old tunnel. At the last moment, the light vanished, and the train could be heard roaring through the new passage.

One of the strangest and most horrific experiences occurred as Sumner led a group to clear land for a camp. In thick woods, he encountered "a death stench, the smell of rotted human flesh." The powerful odor was only sensed by Sumner, not by others beside him. "Since that time many others have smelled it," Sumner claimed, five or six at a time, but on every occasion when some people detected the sickening stench, there were others who could not. That phenomenon is common to many paranormal experiences.

The foul odor of decaying flesh is detected by about one-third of all visitors to the site, Sumner stated. One day, a woman repeatedly smelled fresh coffee boiling nearby, and Sumner caught whiffs of it as well. A ghostly, grinning Confederate revealed himself to Sumner as the soldier held a cup of coffee under the woman's nose. Suddenly, the lady screamed, and the group saw that her nose was bright red.

Another bit of Tunnel Hill weirdness is the phantom campfires. It was a cold, windy December night when Sumner and another man observed campfires on a nearby hillside. They hiked up the ridge to within seventy-five feet of the fires and observed two sets of gray uniformed legs and a pair of hands extended toward the warmth of the fire. "As we approached the fire, the legs disappeared without a trace." Spooked, the men executed a hasty tactical withdrawal. The campfires disappeared until they reached the bottom of the hill, when they spontaneously reignited. The fires burned for two and a half hours.

The fun was not over that night. Sumner retired for the evening but noticed that occasionally the high wind would abruptly cease. "It would get dead still. That's when I heard the footsteps. It got scary that night." He also witnessed ghostly camp guards then and on other occasions.

"I've seen soldier ghosts walk around the perimeter of the camp in spring, around a big fog that rises up that time of the year on the battlefield," Sumner continued. "It's a circular type of fog that surrounds the camp. They just walk around the edge of the fog like camp guards securing their posts. I've also seen some of them trying to get in, and that gets scary, but they haven't ever really bothered us."

A reenactor was sitting in a gun position when another man joined him. The reenactor turned to greet the newcomer only to watch the figure dissolve. Other reenactors walking along a road found a Union soldier asleep on the roadside with his head lying on his pack. They quietly passed, and then glanced back to find that the Federal had disappeared. These phantoms are definitely human in shape, but their faces are always indistinct.

Sumner constructed a fort and named it Key's Battery Fort for a Civil War officer he had studied. He was amazed when a local historian informed him that the reenactor fort was constructed on the site of an original artillery position, one that had officially been called Key's Battery Fort. Sumner, who had no prior knowledge of those facts, was shocked. "Strange parallels continue to amaze us as we research the area history," he said.

Many other paranormal experiences have occurred at Tunnel Hill. The haints bang pans, whack logs against trees and scream from the woods at night. A group saw a lantern float through the area, a frequent psychic experience called a ghost light.

Sumner believes that he knows why Civil War ghosts appear at Tunnel Hill. "Ghosts have to remind everybody, 'Hey, we suffered here.' If you're sincere, they pretty much leave you alone. If not, they try to run you off. If you don't hold reverence, they aren't always pleasant. I've seen people run out of the woods screaming."

The spirits, Confederate and Union alike, want their valor to be remembered. They desire that we learn their history and avoid repeating the same mistakes. Sumner acknowledged that reenactors are often drawn into the past, but "when groups of people see the same things, it's pretty clear something is going on."

On March 16, 2002, several members of the Foundation for Paranormal Research (FPR) met Sumner at Tunnel Hill. The team gathered in the afternoon and pitched camp, then Ken gave the squad a tour of past ghostly activity sites, "places where eerie feelings were present and where the most significant appearances and odors were met," Sumner wrote, particularly the post of the "sentry." Sumner hoped that the many unusual experiences he had encountered could be proven to be natural or paranormal or a result of his own emotions.

Early in the night, the group snapped photos that would reveal a number of orbs and mists, but the weird stuff started later. Olivia Newton captured an electronic voice phenomenon (EVP) on her tape recorder. A male voice was heard saying, "Sleep…sleep…can't sleep," or "See…see…can't see." Personally I heard the "sleep" version.

Immediately after this, Olivia's field strength meter (FSM) started shrieking, "indicating a strong electromagnetic field surrounding it," she wrote. Sumner rushed in and addressed the entity, instructing it to beep once for "no" and twice for "yes." The ghost cooperated, "something that surely has never happened before," Newton recorded, and the group was "shocked at the implications."

Sumner not only communicated with the sentry that night, but he also detected its presence and tracked its movements. At one point, he informed Donna Yavelak that the presence was to his right and urged her to snap a photo. She did, capturing two dark orbs. Sumner redirected her attention, and the second picture revealed a large white orb along the route the sentry often takes. The next photo was of the branches of a tree, where other orbs,

Georgia's most thoroughly haunted Civil War locale is Tunnel Hill, where reenactors and ghost hunters have encountered substantial paranormal activity.

large and small, both close to the ground and higher among the branches, appeared on film. Two photos revealed "ectoplasmic mists" hanging over the area.

Newton was exhausted or ill from exploring the area that night (a not uncommon experience—paranormal phenomena often drain energy from batteries and people) and lay down in her tent beside the FSM, which then erupted.

Sumner, believing that the FSM emission was "an attempt to communicate," asked if the spirit was a soldier. The sound increased in volume, and there were two beeps. He ascertained the entity's name to be Thomas (or Tom) or William Yancy. Sumner asked if Tom wanted to have a cup of coffee by the fire. Tom beeped yes, and Sumner left the tent, feeling "something" follow him. Sumner filled a cup for Tom and one for himself.

Jennifer and Donna Yavelak sat at the fire, looking along a road to the southeast as an electrical storm occasionally lighted the scene. One lightning flash "illuminated for a split second the standing form of a man in a gray uniform standing beside one of the trucks…a Confederate soldier," Sumner wrote of this experience, which he did not personally witness. It might have been the visible spirit of Tom Yancy. A grandson of Sumner's has viewed two Confederates during the daytime at Tunnel Hill.

The FSM indicated that Tom had wandered off, but a few minutes later, the machine emitted a louder sound. Sumner reentered the tent and initiated contact with this new entity. It was not Tom, and it informed Sumner that it was evil. The fresh battery in a flashlight drained when a question was answered. This spirit "was defiant, would not leave and displayed arrogance when the name of Christ was mentioned," Ken wrote. When it refused to depart when ordered to do so, he declared that he would no longer talk to the spirit and left the tent.

Sumner was informed that twenty-three spirits haunted the field, at least two evil and one "dangerous to humans." He believes that there was "an intense desire…to communicate in any way they can." He intends to continue this line of research, feeling that it is important.

When the event started, Sumner had requested the entities "to show themselves in small ways," and that "brought out the most intense display of occurrences in a single night" that he had ever experienced or heard of in nine years of research. Sumner concluded by stating his belief that his major question had been answered—the experiences had not originated in his imagination.

Among the other manifestations encountered was the smell of garbage, which sickened Newton; an area of unnatural fog where the smell and sound of horses were detected; the pushing of people; the sightings of orbs and shadow beings; and faint voices chanting "Olivia" and "Newton." In other areas, a cellphone vanished, a roll of film disappeared from one researcher's hand and one woman experienced energy fields that felt like spider webs.

Demon Ghosts

The evil spirits have not disappeared. After Sumner survived a serious operation on his heart and made a visit to Tunnel Hill several weeks later, a spirit appeared as a witch. "The intent I got was that she wanted to kill me," recorded Corrina Underwood in *Haunted History: Atlanta and North Georgia*. "I felt she had the intention to do me serious harm."

Sumner, feeling weakened, left Tunnel Hill. He returned a week later to again encounter the entity. Sumner informed the being that it had not harmed him the first time they met, and it would not now. On several occasions since, the witch has been spotted at a distance.

During a 2003 reenactment, a man heard footfalls outside his tent one night and went out to investigate. What he encountered was a strange darkness above. The rattled reenactor threw wood on his campfire and lit his candles. At dawn, he informed Sumer that he would never approach that spot again, even during the day.

At several other events, Sumner and FPR members have felt foreboding presences and detected evil, disembodied laughter.

Wildfire

The extraordinary paranormal phenomena manifested at Tunnel Hill encouraged the Foundation for Paranormal Research to continue its investigation. In April and November 2002, a new and unusual wrinkle emerged at Tunnel Hill: phantom horses.

Hundreds of thousands of horses were used by both armies during the war, their work indispensable to the cavalry, artillery, ambulances and supply wagons, as well as to officers and their couriers. Many faithful horses succumbed to battle wounds, disease, exhaustion and starvation. It should come as no surprise that their psychic presence lives on at battlefields.

Not only is there an equine ghost at Tunnel Hill, Ken Sumner also believes that he has identified the individual animal. The reenactment fort erected on the property occupies the site of Key's Battery, erected here during the winter of 1863–64, and it was also the headquarters of Captain Thomas J. Key. In November 1864, his favorite gelding, Black Satin, which had served him for years, died within the fort and was buried nearby.

The April operation, led by Jennifer McElhannon, met around a campfire before teams dispersed with specific assignments. One member detected the odor of horse manure, although there were no horses within a mile of them. She later smelled and heard horses in woods near the fort and was forced "to vacate the site due to [an allergic] reaction" to the horses. She retired to her vehicle, fifty yards distant, and her "intense respiratory distress" disappeared.

The April campfire was surrounded by "evidence of fields of energy [that] produced photographs of an abundance of orbs, including spirit interaction with the foundation members," the report noted. "These presences seemed to follow the teams as soon as the dispersal was made, leaving the hill top almost sterile or devoid of sensed energy." Photographic mists "seemed to literally follow orders," and in several pictures, some members could discern a horse.

In November, David Chastain and a companion set off down a wooded slope equipped with a digital camera, a vision scope and maps. The first half-hour passed quietly. "Suddenly," Chastain wrote, "I heard leaves being disturbed behind me." He turned and by moonlight saw "a disturbance throwing the leaves up in a straight line as it made its way toward me." The phenomenon originated fifteen yards away and covered that distance in just a few seconds. Chastain "felt every hair on my arms, legs, and back of my head stand straight up." Cursing, he leaped several feet into the air, and the activity immediately stopped directly in front of him. He took to his knees and quickly searched the leaves for an explanation of the phenomenon but found nothing. Chastain, a Gulf War Marine Corps veteran and city policeman, had rarely been so startled, writing, "I've never had such a fight or flight reaction." His digital shots included a definite image of a ghostly human and a very interesting, highly textured orb.

The November experience, according to Sumner, produced "sounds of a horse walking on the gravel road, of tack clattering or rattling and the odor of fresh horse manure."

Several group members snapped away, and the results were "breathtaking." Although the phenomenon was invisible to human eyes, digital and video cameras "showed some astonishing forms." Three different images "captured what appeared to be a horse in various degrees of manifestation." One seemed to show a spectral rider; another depicts a spirited, rearing horse; and the third "filled the field of view with an eerie mist, with the perfect form of a black horse appearing as solid as if he were standing within yards!" One picture appears to depict a man holding a sword. A multitude of orbs and mists were captured in the tunnel, camp, woods and overhead in trees, and lights were spotted on the mountain. Sumner often states his belief that two spirits follow him around the site, and photos tend to support his belief.

At one point, a participant "reported having an intense feeling of presences or pressure at a certain point near the camp as he emerged from the field."

No phantom voices were detected, in contrast to the previous exploration here, which Sumner attributed to "strong electrical fields" due to a "severe electric storm" at the earlier effort. The organization has noted that "more intense paranormal activity" occurs in cool weather. Also, having new members there, "without preconceived notions, often results in some extraordinary evidence."

"Some of our researchers have been clawed in the middle of a field," Sumner told Alan Brown in *Stories from the Haunted South*. "I've made the mist move back and forth, depending on what I told the entities to do…It's been rather eerie."

"GrayGhost" informed the website Ghost Hounds that he is a cavalry reenactor who participated in several events at Tunnel Hill during the mid-1990s. "I have seen the Napoleon 12 lb. cannons misfire a lot for no reason there. The horses always act really jumpy and spooky there, like they sense something in the woods around the area. That is why I really don't like this reenactment."

GrayGhost heard a thirdhand report of a reenactor at the tunnel who was having an interesting conservation with a man dressed as a Civil War–era railroad conductor. After fifteen minutes, the man was briefly interrupted, and when he turned back to his new companion, he found that "the conductor had vanished." No one had knowledge of a conductor reenactor being at the event.

On February 21, 2004, Drew Hester was part of a FPR research effort. The night was cold, just thirty-eight degrees, and Hester explored the southern end of the field and along a tree line. He encountered a number of cold and warm spots and took photos when he initially encountered each cold place. This philosophy garnered a large orb in a field and another above tents pitched by reenactors. He captured four orbs, an ectoplasmic phenomenon and a blue line formation.

After an hour, Hester reconnected with others and discovered that he had missed the primary show that night. One group had encountered three ghosts that so frightened them that one member threw his lantern at the apparitions. All the witnesses swore that the entities "looked malnourished, tired, scared and, most of all, cold." Not a fit night out for man nor ghost, apparently. Hester and others ventured to that area, encountering cold spots and photographing orbs in the woods.

Hester made a coffee and food run to Dalton and returned for a personal tour of the tunnel with Ken Sumner. There, Hester photographed an ectoplasm. His experiences that night convinced him that the activity at Tunnel Hill is both intelligent and residual.

According to Georgiana C. Kotarski in *Ghosts of the Southern Tennessee Valley*, Tunnel Hill historian Larry Thornton does not personally believe in ghosts but has certainly heard his fair share of stories. Casualties had been treated at the Clisby-Austin House as far back as Shiloh in the spring of 1862, the most prominent patient being John B. Hood. Thornton believes that Hood's leg was amputated here by surgeon T.G. Richardson, the leg being buried in the nearby family cemetery. Hood died in 1879 of yellow fever in New Orleans, but some believe that his spirit lingers in Tunnel Hill. He spends most days recuperating in the east second-floor bedroom, peering out a window and rocking. An empty rocking chair in the room regularly creaks. If the chair is moved, Hood relocates it back to his window.

Angie Madden is a graphic artist who cofounded Paranormal Investigators of Georgia (PIG) in 2002. The team spent a night inside the railroad tunnel. Turning to look at the closed gate, "I could swear that I saw someone walking back and forth in front of the gate," she told Alan Brown in *Ghost Hunters of the South*. What she saw was a shadow in profile wearing a soldier's hat.

Many reenactors and visitors see ghostly Confederate figures, single or in pairs, standing still or walking around. Sumner sometimes sees figures that others do not, and at other times he cannot see what others do, including a skeptic who was converted on the spot. While at Tunnel Hill playing ball with his grandson, the lad mentioned two strangers standing nearby who were not visible to Sumner. The description of the men's clothing revealed them to be phantom Confederates. At one event, a reenactor observed an "extra" man eating at their table—no one else could see him.

The FPR spent the night of July 12, 2008, at Tunnel Hill. Bev wrote that she never leaves the site "without having some kind of unexplained experience." As the team sat in a circle at the camp, a white mist rolled in. Then Bev saw "a black silhouette of a human running towards the woods" directly in front of her. The being, only visible from the thighs up, looked to be running and took two steps before vanishing. The black figure was quite distinct against the mist. The night at Tunnel Hill left Bev with a "respect and empathy to those of the past who gave their lives in that horrible war."

In the early morning hours, four participants were in a field when "we all heard a high pitched, loud, shrill scream," wrote Connie. Two men felt that it was an entity that was twenty-three years old. Several orbs were photographed at that time, one particularly "bright and perfectly circular."

The railroad tunnel, the Clisby-Austin House and additional property are being developed by Whitfield County. Check with the Tunnel Hill Historical Foundation for developments.

Georgia's Ghost Train

The "Great Locomotive Chase" thundered down the Western & Atlantic Railroad from Kennesaw to a point several miles north of Ringgold. In 1881, *Railroad* magazine printed an account of what might have been a ghostly reenactment of that historic event:

> *A mysterious apparition was seen one night recently. The narrator was walking the track of the Western & Atlantic Railroad about two miles from Dalton when he discovered the headlight of a locomotive approaching around a curve. Strange to say, he heard no noise as the train came speedily on.*
>
> *Presently he stepped from the track and waited for it to pass. No noise attended the engine's approach. As he came opposite he noticed that the whole machinery had a ghostly phantom-like appearance. At the throttle stood a pale, wide-eyed engineer, while a specter-like fireman was pulling the bell rope. But no sound came from the bell. All this he observed as the train rushed past him like a shadow!*

"A Georgia Volunteer," by Mary Ashley Townsend

"The bramble wrestled with the weed
Upon the lonely mound;
The simple headboard rudely writ
Had rotted to the ground;
I raised it with a reverent hand,
From dust its words to clear,
But time had blotted all but these,
'A Georgia Volunteer.'"

RESACA

Resaca was the site of the first major battle between Sherman and Johnston. For several days, May 13–15, the armies hammered each other in the valley of Camp Creek. Neither side won a victory, but Sherman used his superior forces to outflank Johnston, forcing the Confederates to retreat closer to

Resaca, site of the largest battle during the Atlanta Campaign, has a multitude of paranormal manifestations.

Atlanta. After the battle, local women buried the Confederate dead, but unfortunately, many were unidentified.

On the last anniversary date of Resaca (May 15), a group devoted to the study and remembrance of the Civil War arrived at Resaca to decorate the graves of Confederates gathered at the Resaca Confederate Cemetery, Georgia's oldest, established in 1866. According to *Skeletons of the Civil War*, as they entered the cemetery, the wind ceased blowing and birds stopped singing. In the distance, a sound like yelping was heard, the sound growing more and more distant, fading out about thirty minutes later. The group agreed that the sound had been male voices screaming the "Rebel yell" en masse.

The State of Georgia has purchased a substantial portion of the Resaca battlefield, and a historic park will be developed.

"What fights he fought, what wounds he wore,
And all unknown to fame;
Remember on his lonely grave
There is not e'en a name!
That he fought well, and bravely, too,

And held his country dear
We know, else he had never been
'A Georgia Volunteer.'"'

BARNSLEY GARDENS

Where the Dead Walk

Nearly everyone interested in ghost stories is familiar with Barnsley Gardens, which sits in rural splendor between Adairsville and Kingston. It was to be the grand plantation of Godfrey Barnsley, an English immigrant who grew rich in the cotton trade. In 1840, he purchased 3,600 acres in northern Georgia to remove his beloved wife, Julia, and their children from the deadly illnesses of coastal Georgia. Here they raised a grand Italianate manor house, Woodlands, with extensive gardens. Unfortunately, ill fortune dogged the family—some link it to the curse of a removed Cherokee chief. Julia died in 1845, four of their six children died young and Godfrey lost his fortune through investments in the Confederate cause. Worse yet, in May 1864, one-third of Sherman's force, the Army of the Tennessee under Major General James B. McPherson, marched through the plantation.

Godfrey died in 1875, and in 1905, a tornado ripped the roof off the beautiful mansion. In 1935, one of Godfrey's grandsons killed his own brother in the detached kitchen, where the family then lived.

The property was purportedly cursed by Cherokees who were forced to leave their land in 1836, but an alternate story has Native Americans, believing the curious acorn-shaped hill to be already condemned, advising Barnsley to build elsewhere. The history of the estate certainly suggests that the land was damned. Thankfully, during the 1980s, Woodlands' fortunes rebounded as the house and grounds were purchased by a wealthy European man who established a grand golf resort. In 1988, the new owner transported a group of Native Americans from North Carolina and Oklahoma to bless the plantation. That allegedly lifted the plague of disasters.

Legend has Godfrey regularly communicating with Julia's ghost during the period separating their deaths, and reportedly she continues to stroll through her beloved gardens. Julia was particularly fond of the twelve-foot-tall fountain situated amid the boxwoods. Granddaughter Julie B. Saylor commonly encountered her there, and Barnsley often wrote of feeling his wife's presence

The remains of the grand estate at Barnsley are still haunted by dead residents and a Confederate officer killed during combat here.

Spectral figures of long-deceased residents are seen in the exotic gardens at Barnsley.

everywhere on the grounds. Julie's uncle, George Barnsley, one of Barnsley's sons who accepted self-imposed exile in Brazil after the war, appeared at the estate on the night he died in South America. At least three other deceased members of the Barnsley family have been seen on the property.

As Federal soldiers approached Barnsley's Gardens in 1864, Confederate colonel Richard G. Earle, a friend of Barnsley's, raced to warn the Englishman of the threat. While riding away, Earle was killed, shot five times by Union soldiers, and fell on a gravel walk in the gardens, surrounded by a hundred varieties of roses, wrote witness Charles W. Willis of Illinois. Earle's troopers, angered, charged and captured one hundred Federals before being driven off by Union reinforcements.

A more likely story is that Earle's First Alabama Cavalry drove a regiment of Union cavalry from the outskirts of Kingston to the main Federal cavalry line at Barnsley's, where Earle was killed near the house by Union private Thomas H. Boner. Earle was buried by the women of the family on the terrace near the home. Whatever story you prefer, Earle's ghost, clad in a Confederate uniform, has often been seen in the garden, having apparently found his paradise. A prominent landmark at Barnsley's is Earle's grave, marked near the kitchen wing by a small stone that bears his name and rank. After the war, relatives in Alabama arrived and attempted unsuccessfully to exhume the body and return it to his home soil.

According to Chris Wrangler in *Ghost Stories of Georgia*, Addie, Julie's daughter, also witnessed Colonel Earle, wearing a gray uniform, with a lost look on his face, in the garden near the site of his death.

Of further Civil War note is an incident that occurred when archaeologist Gilbert Smith excavated artifacts from the site of a Federal campsite. As his team completed its work, it heard the haunting sounds of a ghostly bugler performing taps.

ALLATOONA PASS

"HOLD THE FORT, FOR I AM COMING," BY PHILIP P. BLISS

Ho, my comrades, see the signal,
Waving in the sky!
Reinforcements now appearing,
Victory is nigh.

"Hold the fort, for I am coming,"
Jesus signals still;
Wave the answer back to Heaven
"By thy grace we will."
See the mighty host advancing,
Satan leading on,
Mighty men around us falling,
Courage almost gone!
See the glorious banner waving,
Hear the trumpet blow!
In our Leader's name we'll triumph,
Over every foe
Fierce and long the battle rages,
But our help is near,
Onward comes our great Commander,
Cheer, my comrades, cheer.
"Hold the fort, for I am coming,"
Jesus signals still,
Wave the answer back to heaven,
"By thy grace we will."

After Sherman evacuated Atlanta, Confederate general John B. Hood attempted to lure the Federals out of the city by invading Tennessee. On October 5, 1864, a strong Southern force repeatedly assaulted Union fortifications at the top of a railroad cut at Allatoona. The Federal force barely survived, but both sides suffered heavy casualties. The action inspired the great old hymn "Hold the Fort, for I Am Coming," by noted songwriter Philip P. Bliss.

On October 28, 1934, the *Atlanta Journal Magazine* published a story about E.L. (Polly) Milan, a man who started his railroading career in 1877. Born on May 25, 1861, two months before the first battle of the Civil War, he was seventy-three years old and had worked on the railroad for fifty-seven years, rising to the position of engineer. Three years after going to work on the railroad, at the age of nineteen, he saw the ghost of Allatoona Pass:

> *"I've been in several bad wrecks," he testified, "but running into that spook was worse than all my wrecks."*
>
> *As a young man, Milan worked the brakes, a hazardous job that required men to turn brakes located between train cars as locomotives*

> *thundered down the mountains. "Air brakes were unknown and the track was crooked and treacherous through the lonesome and foreboding mountains," Milan related, "but nothing happened to give me a fright until the night I met the ghost."*
>
> *"We were coming south with a little freight train and had topped a grade to dip into Allatoona, when it was discovered that the train had broken into two," the old engineer continued. "It was shortly before midnight, and I was ordered to go back and flag a train that was following us. With my pistol in my right hand and my red and white lanterns in the left, I hit the ground and ran back up the hill. I stopped in the middle of a cut that was about 60 feet deep and some 400 feet long.*
>
> *"There was a soldier's grave at the north end of this dark and scary looking cavern and I had heard of strange things having been heard and seen there. So I stopped in the middle of this cut because I did not want to pass this grave. There I stood in the dark, my pistol in my hand. The train had coupled up and gone on, leaving me alone out there in the mountains where anything could happen in those days.*
>
> *"Well, a few minutes after the exhaust of my train had faded into the night, I was horrified to see something that looked like a man with a sheet thrown over him, come out of the dark, near the north end of the cut, and slowly approach me. Scared almost to death, and not knowing what to do, I just stood there and watched the 'thing' come toward me. When it got within sixty feet of where I stood, it slumped wearily down to the ties.*
>
> *"It just sat there, as though tired out, while I pondered what to do. Finally I spoke to it, but it said nothing. I spoke again, but only the sound of my voice echoed in the dismal cut. I didn't know what to do! The lanterns were jingling in my hand and my teeth were rattling like dried peas in a pod.*
>
> *"Then something seemed to shove me toward the thing. When I reached it, I touched it with the back of my pistol hand. I'll never forget the sensation as long as I live! It was cold and still and in less time than it takes to tell it, I was tearing wildly down that track. I ran over a mile and a half before the train that I was to flag overtook me!"*

In conclusion, Milan said, "I don't know what it was. Lots of railroad men claim to have seen 'boogers' in that cut."

The first encounters with train ghosts had occurred a decade earlier, according to the *Savannah Morning News* of December 9, 1872, just seven years after war's end:

> *For some months, railroaders, conductors, engineers and brakemen, have been noticing between Tilton and Allatoona that when their respective freight trains would enter on to that portion of the track named, that their number would be reinforced by* An Extra Train Hand*,…This individual appears suddenly on top of the freight cars, takes a seat, and remains there for many miles, then the unknown brakeman disappears. Conductors, seeing him, have often gone out to collect his fare, but on nearing him, he would vanish like mist. One night an engineer on a freight train plainly saw* The Ghostly Brakeman *seated on top of the third car from his engine, and determined to settle the vexed question as to who he was, and accordingly left his engine in charge of the fireman, and proceeded at once towards the mysterious object. The engineer approached cautiously, with both eyes fixed on the forming of the man, but as he neared his ghostship, he gradually* Faded from View*, leaving the engineer completely bewildered, but who still tried to unravel the suddenness of his disappearance by passing over the entire train and looking in every place which was capable of concealing a man, but nowhere was the man visible. The engineer turned around in despair, and as he cast his eye toward the engine, which was swift in speed, there sat the object of his search, unterrified and full of life, on the same identical spot where he first discovered him. It was all incomprehensibly strange and unaccountable to the engineer, but his intrepid courage never failed him, and he again went towards him, and as he approached, again the apparition* Dissolved Itself into Nothing*. The engineer passed on to his engine and on looking back, there sat perched upon the car box the same unknown being, where he remained until the train had left many miles in the distance, then his ghostship disappeared, probably to re-enact on the next passing train the same scenes. His appearance on the top of trains has become a matter of indifference among the railroad men, and all effort to find out who he is has ceased.*

The soldier's grave has generated a traditional ghost light story. A mysterious illuminated orb is seen bobbing along the railroad at night, reputedly the spirit soldier carrying a lantern in search of long-vanished comrades, and balls of light flit around the grave. A variation has the phantom soldier's ghost dog running alongside passing engines before stopping at his master's grave.

Bruce W. Burns, director of Historical Research for the Foundation for Paranormal Research, has written a good overview of the battle and

The Civil War railroad passed through Allatoona Gap, where a desperate battle was fought in October 1864. Casualties seem to linger.

an interesting investigation report. He camped in Allatoona Pass before it became a protected and promoted historical site and wrote of his experiences:

> *At night (sometimes in the daytime if quiet enough), you can hear what sounds like thunder, which is actually the sound of civil war artillery followed by the unmistakable smell of burned black powder. You can hear battle cries and soldiers rushing thru the underbrush. On occasion you can see soldiers running where the railroad tracks were. A group of friends and I used to camp out there back in the late '70s and early '80s. One member of our group wandered off by herself down the old rail bed and was approached by a man in a Union officer's garb who asked her if she'd seen his horse. When she asked him what happened to his arm (his right arm was missing and the sleeve of his uniform was tattered and bloody) he replied that he must have taken a hit, then he vanished.*

The Hat Trick

On October 30, 2004, Burns and FPR members Tina, Rick, Bev, Jen and Russell landed at the site via Lake Allatoona. To mark the spot where they intersected the trail, they placed an empty cigarette pack on a limb, although Tina, a staunch University of Georgia fan, told Bruce he should leave his Notre Dame hat instead. Bruce wrote:

> *While descending the stairs from the Star Fort I noticed my hat missing. I believed that I must have lost it down in the cut because I remembered feeling my shirt tugged on when we were walking thru the cut so I kept an eye out for it… but I didn't see it when we were walking back.*
>
> *As we approached the spot where we entered the trail from the lake, I saw the cigarette pack and remarked, "There's the cigarette pack." And Tina, who was looking around with a flashlight said, "And there's your hat." My hat was lying on the ground directly under the limb with the cigarette pack.*
>
> *Initially I believed that I MUST have left my hat there and forgotten it but later on, after reviewing the video, I realized that wasn't the case. The video footage shot up at the Star Fort clearly shows that my hat was on my head at the time.*
>
> *Bev, Jen, and Tina all had the "spider web" sensation at times. Tina had something pass through her and completely take her breath at the original grave of the Unknown Hero and Bev photographed a huge orb hovering over Russell in the same spot moments later. As we walked thru the cut everyone sensed something moving along with us along the ridgeline of the eastern side of the cut, and I caught a brief bit of movement on video.*

The most haunted part of the battlefield was the point where the old rail bed curved west. There, as Bruce wrote:

> *1) Most everybody smelled kerosene.*
> *2) Just after that, most everybody smelled burned gunpowder.*
> *3) Some smelled rotting flesh.*
> *4) Most of us had the distinct feeling that we weren't alone.*
>
> *And then "something" scratched Jennifer's back and sides. I captured it on video—the whelps formed and clarified right before our eyes. Just after Jen got clawed we all felt an urgent need to vacate the area, so we did.*

Red Top Mountain State Park is now responsible for the Allatoona Pass battlefield. Samantha Wiley, exhibit guide at the park, is not surprised by reports of hauntings at Allatoona. "With that much bloodshed, and anxiety and frustration and anger," she said, "there's got to be something." While she personally has experienced nothing usual there, "it's not that far off a statement to believe that hauntings are going on out there." Even she finds it "pretty creepy back there."

Across the road from the railroad cut is a white, two-story house with double porches. The Clayton-Mooney House dates to the early 1830s, ten years before the railroad arrived, when workers boarded in the house. During the Battle of Allatoona, it was first a Federal headquarters and later a field hospital for both armies. A number of bullets penetrated the wooden structure, and twenty-one Confederate battle dead are buried in the backyard. The family of Diane Mooney has owned the house since 1951, and she has spent most of her life there. Dennis moved in after their wedding in 1979, and both have experienced paranormal phenomenon, including kitchen cabinet doors opening and closing by themselves. Late one night, a motion-activated light in the hall switched on when no one was present, and the Mooneys heard phantom footsteps on the stairs.

When former Confederate colonel Thomas Spencer visited the Clayton House in the 1920s, wooden grave markers still stood behind the residence. He had a marble marker commemorating the twenty-one Confederates on the property placed in front of the house.

In 1994, Diane and Dennis decided to erect a barn on the property and wanted to plot the graves in order to avoid disturbing them. Through the Etowah Valley Historical Society, they contacted Carl Etheridge, a ranger and historian with the Army Corps of Engineers. Among other techniques for detecting burials, Carl employed divining rods, which he does not believe are in any way supernatural tools. Soil excavated for graves has a different magnetic pull than undisturbed earth. Diane thought that the graves were in the woods, but in the backyard, Carl picked up "definite rod movements in a patterned row time after time," and he placed a flag at each site. Being a little skeptical, Diane recalled where they had buried her horse when she was a child. She asked Carl to locate Flame's resting place, and within fifteen minutes, he had. To substantiate Carl's grave sites, soil scrapings were taken. Analysis at each found high concentrations of calcium and small bone fragments pronounced human by archaeologists. The twenty-one Confederate graves, and also old Flame's, soon had traditional marble headstones.

The spirit of an unknown Confederate buried along the track near Allatoona Pass was encountered by a railroad worker decades ago.

The battlefield of Allatoona Pass, including the dramatic railroad cut and hilltop fortifications, can be visited during daylight hours.

"The Battle of Allatoona Pass," by Sergeant Major Solomon T. Flint, Seventh Illinois

Sweep It Over the Hills of Georgia
To the Mountains of the North,
Teach the Coward and the Doubter
What the Blood of Man Is Worth.
Hail the Flag You Pass!
Let Its Stained and Tattered Mass
Tell the Story of the Terror and the Glory,
Of the Battle of the Allatoona Pass.

Saltpeter Cave and the Kingston Confederate Hospital

Near Kingston in western Bartow County is Saltpeter Cave, where the Confederate government harvested considerable quantities of saltpeter, one of the primary ingredients of gunpowder, before Sherman destroyed the facility. The formation is ancient, and explorers have found the remains of long-vanished prehistoric beasts in its corridors. Although this tale predates the Civil War, perhaps to Native American times, it might have been experienced by Confederate work crews. Visitors to the cave have reported experiencing the sounds of footsteps and cries for help, as well as chills and generally weird feelings. According to the Etowah Valley Historical Society, a "mysterious sing-song humming of a woman's voice [is] often heard in and around the cave." The latter phenomenon started after a band of Cherokee Indians lost a battle with the Creeks and was pursued into the cave, from which many never returned.

Kingston was a major Confederate hospital center before the armies passed through. On the southern edge of town is a large Confederate cemetery where screams, cries for help and footsteps are heard and chills and odd feelings are detected late at night.

NEW HOPE CHURCH

The Hell Hole

Sherman's massive army started into Georgia in May 1864. He was blocked repeatedly by Johnston, but each time, Sherman used his numbers to flank the Confederates and force Johnston to retreat closer to Atlanta. This dance was repeated at Dalton, Resaca and Adairsville until Sherman encountered the Allatoona Mountains south of the Etowah River near Cartersville. Stymied by strong Confederate fortifications in the mountains, he wisely elected to avoid them. Sherman abandoned his railroad supply line and daringly swept far to the southwest, hoping to reach Dallas and the railroad at Kennesaw or Marietta before Johnston could respond.

Johnston was not fooled. To intercept the Federals, he dispatched John B. Hood's corps to take a position at New Hope Church, a crossroads community located in a small clearing. Hood positioned the five thousand infantrymen of A.P. Stewart's division and sixteen artillery pieces behind log breastworks to cover the only approach.

On May 25, Sherman's vanguard, Joseph Hooker's XX Corps, encountered the Confederate position and attacked. It was a slaughter. Hundreds fell before the Southern position, unable to effectively return fire. During the fighting, a terrible thunderstorm engulfed the field. Sheets of rain fell as thunder drowned out the reports of artillery and muskets, and dramatic bolts of lightning streaked the sky.

Federal wounded sought to escape the Confederate and natural storms by crawling into a ravine. It was said that the volume of their moans and screams were heard above the storm raging overhead. Union soldiers remembered this slaughter as the Hell Hole.

The Hell Hole Revisited

Beverly M. DuBose Jr. and Sidney C. Kerksis were two of the most respected Civil War historians in the nation. DuBose, a successful insurance businessman married to Coca-Cola heiress Frances Woodruff, spent much time and considerable money collecting Civil War artifacts. Before his death, DuBose donated a world-class collection to the Atlanta Historical Society, where it makes up a considerable portion of the museum's holdings. He also wrote a number of articles describing Civil War artifacts and how to collect them. Kerksis spent his career in the army, serving in World War II and Korea. He assisted famed Georgia historian Wilbur G. Kurtz in researching and placing the hundreds of historical markers that dot the state's highways. Kerksis also wrote a highly regarded volume on military belt buckles and plates.

These were not ordinary relic collectors, and both men were financially secure and had national reputations to uphold. Certainly, neither had reason to concoct a ghost story. But in the last years of their lives, they repeated the following story to anyone who would listen. DuBose and Kerksis never committed the tale to paper, but Bill Erquitt, once curator of the outstanding Civil War displays at the Atlanta Historical Society, heard the story firsthand on many occasions and wrote the story for *Blue & Gray* magazine.

Sometime in the early to mid-1960s, DuBose and Kerksis drove to New Hope Church to search for relics on the battlefield, particularly in the ravine, where the Civil War landscape would have been little changed in the previous century. They asked permission to search the property from a farmer whose family had held the land since before the Civil War. Their farmhouse had been damaged during the fighting. The owner gladly gave his approval—maybe they would clear away some of the Civil War metal that still damaged his farming equipment. He left for town as the collectors headed for the depression. At that point, Kerksis remembered that it was May 25, the anniversary of the battle. As far as either could recollect, it may have been the 100th anniversary of the battle.

The pair found a collectors' paradise. Other relic hunters had apparently overlooked the area, and erosion left numerous buckles, canteens, bayonets, shells and bullets exposed on the surface. They even found leather gear, which normally would have deteriorated from the passage of time.

After a while, one of the men noticed the smell of decaying meat. He told his buddy that one of the farmer's cows must have stumbled into the ravine and died. The stench intensified, but they could not locate the dead animal. Suddenly, the day's perfect weather disappeared, replaced with black storm clouds. Darkness enveloped the ravine as thunder boomed and lightning split the heavens.

Then one man discerned a sound and pointed it out to his companion. Erquitt described it as "a wail, then some moans, like a weird howling, then what seemed a chorus of agony." The sounds seemed very close. Sheets of rain poured from the sky, thunder crashed ever louder and lightning illuminated the landscape in brief strobes. The cacophony of storm paled before the sounds of agony, and DuBose and Kerksis elected to bolt from the ravine. They stumbled, nearly blinded by the rain, out of the depression and took shelter in a shed, the spectral sounds of suffering following them even there.

The storm ended abruptly, as did the ghastly human noises, as the farmer returned. He took the men into his house and dried their soaked clothing. After several awkward minutes, one of the collectors mentioned the dead cow in the ravine. The farmer gave them a knowing look as he told them he did not allow his cows onto that part of his property, and he rarely visited it himself.

"When I was a boy," he said, "my daddy, like his daddy before him, never let us kids play down there. He always said there was something terrible about the place." Neither collector ever returned to New Hope Church.

In 1864, Union survivors dubbed the battle place "the Hell Hole," and that name was reinforced 112 years later in April 1976, when a DC-9 encountered a sudden storm that shut down one engine. The plane crashed at New Hope, killing seventy-three of eighty passengers, seven

Pickett's Mill was a wilderness battlefield, perfectly preserved today, and it is the scene of ghostly reenactments.

people in a car, a woman in her yard and a man at a store when some shattered gas pumps ignited. The wreckage was concentrated at the center of the Hell Hole.

DuBose's son, Beverly DuBose III, also heard the story many times from his father. "It got absolutely pitch dark," he remembered from his father's description. "The wind blew like hell, lightning and thunder. It rained in sheets. It got very cold." He said the collectors "could feel the suffering of the wounded."

"Dad spent days and nights on battlefields all over the South and never had another experience like this," DuBose told the *Atlanta Journal Constitution* in October 1996, "and he was not given to flights of fancy."

Be aware that a number of writers have appropriated this story and crafted their own personal, fictionalized version of it. What you just read is the true, original tale—accept no substitutes.

The intersection at New Hope Church is marked today by historical markers and monuments, two churches and a cemetery with gravestones that sheltered soldiers from enemy fire. Some acres of the battlefield are being preserved.

PICKETT'S MILL

The Battle Goes on Forever

Unable to penetrate Confederate lines at New Hope Church, General Sherman continued his flanking move toward Kennesaw, but again he encountered Confederate resistance, this time at Pickett's Mill on May 27. The result was a repeat of New Hope Church. Defeated Federals took shelter in a ravine (a different one than the New Hope Church), but during the night, Confederates charged into the gully, killing or capturing hundreds. The battlefield, little disturbed before it was purchased by the State of Georgia, is nearly pristine, making it one of the most perfectly preserved in the nation. The park is a favorite haunt of reenactors as well as ghosts.

The Moonlit Road is an excellent website dedicated to southern ghost stories. When its creator, Craig Dominey, decided to investigate real Civil War spirits, he consulted Cheri Mohr Drake of the now dissolved Georgia Haunt Hunt Club, headquartered in Athens, and they initially planned to study the battlefield at Chickamauga. However, after examining the Hell Hole stories, they decided to stay closer to home. Dominey studied the notorious ravine but decided that there were too many houses and too much traffic in the area for proper ghost hunting. At Pickett's Mill State Historic Site, he asked park rangers about paranormal incidents on government property. They had heard many ghost stories about the battlefield, particularly near the date of the battle. Dominey made arrangements for himself and Drake to meet a ranger at 8:15 p.m. on October 1.

Traffic and bad directions slowed the intrepid ghost hunters, prompting Drake to suggest that perhaps "whatever we were searching for didn't want us to come, and was throwing obstacles in our path." Drake said such incidents "had happened to her group in the past."

They were an hour late, and the ranger had gone home, but Drake and Dominey decided to investigate the area around the parking lot with her thermal temperature scanner and electromagnetic field detector. At a flicker of abnormality, Drake took photos.

The expedition's gremlin was apparently still at work. Batteries purchased an hour earlier were found to be drained, and the electromagnetic field detector inexplicably failed. Drake had previously commented that ghosts are in the habit of adversely affecting batteries and equipment.

The thermal temperature scanner and camera worked, though, so they swept the field, snapping photos when a "cold spot" was detected. As they approached the woods, "I was hit with what I can only describe as a sense of dread," Dominey recorded. He had intended to enter the woods, but something "made me stop in my tracks."

"Suddenly, deep in the forest, I saw what appeared to be sparks," Dominey continued. At that moment, from the opposite side of the parking area, Drake shouted, "I just saw sparks!"

"It was then that I heard a bizarre sound from deep in the forest," Dominey wrote. "The only way I can describe it is that it sounded like a recording of the moan of a wounded animal, with reverb effects added in a recording studio. This was followed by a sudden *whooshing* sound of something flying through the trees. Truthfully, it sounded like a bullet, again with some bizarre reverb effect."

A Cold Night in Hell

Drake also heard the sound, and both agreed to leave the developing skirmish. They drove to the old cemetery at New Hope Church, where fighting is believed to have occurred.

Approaching the cemetery, Drake assured the spirits that their intentions were friendly and that they only wanted to take photographs. She did this upon entering a cemetery to placate the inhabitants. Dominey soon noted "dramatic temperature drops" of twenty degrees or more and discovered that "this cold spot moved—and moved fast! Once I got a read on a cold spot, I could follow it as it circled around us."

Although the temperature was in the sixties, Drake was standing in a spot so cold her breath could be seen in the flashlight beam. Before leaving the cemetery, they again "saw random sparks."

Photos developed the following day showed one unexplained light and frequent "tiny white lights" that resembled their earlier "sparks."

Spirited Theories, or Hydroelectric Ghosts

According to Drake, not only did a deadly battle occur at Pickett's Mill, but there is also "a little creek or a water source; I've had people tell me that they can't stand to be around the creek that's up there—that's another source of energy that we think entities draw from. So if you've had something terrible happen there where a ghost might [be] or in denial that they are dead, and you have an energy source to draw from, you might feel the effect of that more readily."

Drake proposed that Civil War apparitions could be the result of a "residual haunting," which occurs when the spirit has departed, like "a recording...we put down a voice on magnetic tape, and we put down our image on magnetic videotape." She believed that "a highly charged moment" is made "on these naturally occurring geomagnetic fields." Apparently, the recordings are tripped when the "fields are stronger on this particular day when people might see a bunch of soldiers." Storms like the one that occurred during the battle might be another trigger.

Drake believed that ghosts, or residual hauntings, can occur at "almost any battlefield location in the state...Usually what happens is that people will mistake these ghosts for reenactors until they fade away!"

Reenactors Experience the Real Civil War

In the late 1990s, according to B. Keith Toney in *Battlefield Ghosts*, two reenactors arrived at Pickett's Mill near midnight. Rather than pack their gear through the dark, rainy night to the encampment, they decided to sleep in their truck, parked near the visitors' center and the ravine.

One awoke at 2:00 a.m. to a sound emanating from the ravine. "It sounded kind of like somebody whispering," he told his comrade. Both soon heard something scraping through the underbrush in the nearby historic gully. More whispering was detected, and as the men debated what was happening, they heard massed voices shouting the Rebel yell and a body of men crashing down the slope of the depression. At that time, the men concluded that their buddies were playing war and decided to wait until dawn before joining them.

The reenactors got up early and peered into the ravine. They were puzzled to find no footprints or other marks indicating that anyone had recently ventured into it. The men humped their gear half a mile to the camp and questioned the men in their reenactment unit. Because of the ugly weather, none had left the area the previous night. The reenactment they heard had apparently been the original Confederates of 1864, an event reminiscent of the suffering Federals who had returned to the Hell Hole a few miles away at New Hope Church.

Doorway to Heaven

The ravine at Pickett's Mill was the scene of another bizarre incident on the night of May 27, 1994, the 130th anniversary of the battle. According to Scott McKay, seven or eight people, including a now retired historian at nearby Kennesaw Mountain National Battlefield Park, had received special permission to camp that night in the gully. It was 10:00 p.m., the exact moment of the Confederate attack to clear the ravine of Federals. McKay and the historian were taking turns describing the battle that had occurred there, and he was speaking when "all of a sudden, a silhouette of a door frame faded up (in a blue/green neon caste), hung momentarily, then faded down." McKay hesitated and "then shook it off" and resumed his lecture. Several minutes later, he saw the same apparition but told no one because they "would have thought me delusional."

Next morning around the campfire, one of the group confessed that he had observed the same vision. "Soon everyone spoke up that they had seen it too!"

McKay supposed that the "glow in such a distinct shape was some sort of a passageway," an entrance to the afterlife for the "five hundred Federals violently ending their lives at that spot, so if that sort of a passageway were to exist, that would sure be the place."

On other occasions, witnesses at Pickett's Mill have sighted misty figures that run between trees and disappear.

The State of Georgia Begs to Report

The Georgia State Park system legitimized a number of Civil War ghost stories, using them to attract visitors around Halloween. A state-maintained website described a reenactment at Pickett's Mill in which "a Confederate actor stopped to take a drink of water and noticed a quivering young boy dressed in Union blue cowering as he neared. As the reenactor turned to get a closer look, the boy suddenly disappeared into thin air."

On another occasion, according to the state, several visitors "stopped by the visitor's center to inquire as to where the demonstrations were being held. When the confused staffer tried to inform them that no event was scheduled for that day, the baffled visitors then explained that they had just seen a group of Confederate soldiers crossing the street."

Thousands of unknown Confederate soldiers rest in lonely graves. Perhaps these unidentified souls still roam Georgia's battlefields and hospital sites.

Recently, "a family was hosting a reunion in one of the site's popular group shelters and decided to take a picture of all the women in the family standing in front of the building. Later, when the film was developed, they noticed an interloper lurking in the background, despite the fact that no one was left inside when the picture was taken. Upon closer inspection, they could make out the face of a Civil War soldier through the window of the empty building behind them! Perhaps he was checking the ladies out."

This last story reinforces an earlier incident reported from this area: a photograph taken behind Mount Tabor Church, where Confederate earthworks remain near the New Hope battlefield. No one was present when the picture was snapped, but when it was developed, a distinct image of a Civil War soldier emerged. It is thought to be Lieutenant Colonel John Herrod, severely wounded at the Battle of New Hope Church.

Rodney and Denise are a married Polk County couple who organized the True Paranormal Research Society. On one of their first investigations, they were at Pickett's Mill when they smelled smoke. "What caused that," they asked aloud, and an EVP replied, "Yea, I'm shooting off the bridge"—a bridge that had been destroyed years earlier.

Pickett's Mill, located near Dallas in Paulding County, is an outstanding state historical park.

Dallas

The Long Road Home

In mid-October 1984, *Dallas New Era* reporter Nan McQuillen sat down to talk with ninety-two-year-old Maggie Jasper, who lived on the Cartersville Highway on the outskirts of Dallas. Jasper claimed to have seen ghosts walking along that road when she sat on her front porch, but only between September and mid-November. They mostly walked alone, but not always, on the grassy medium of the highway, always at dusk or a little later. The spirits never spoke but responded as if they heard comments directed at them. The ghosts had also been seen by Jasper's children and neighbors.

All the ghosts turned into the old Hucklemeir homeplace, an ancient, boarded-up two-story house. It looked haunted, and most locals considered it so and avoided the structure. Jasper said that she was one of the few locals who would venture into the creepy dwelling.

Jasper told the story of Melanie Hucklemeir, a beautiful young woman who was born in the house and died there. "That was a mighty sad thing to happen," she said before telling the story. Melanie, described by Jasper as having "long blond hair with large round brown eyes," fell in love before the Civil War with Robert Habersham, a handsome man from Rome. The two planned to marry after Robert returned from fighting for the Confederacy. Before he left, Robert often rode his horse from Rome to visit Melanie. As she waited for the end of the war, Melanie spent many hours stitching her white satin wedding dress.

When the war ended, Robert never appeared, and none of his comrades knew his fate. Soon, every eligible man in the area was trying to win Melanie's hand. "There wasn't one who didn't fall in love with her," Jasper said. The young girl's suitors were so fervent that one man was shot to death and a second was badly maimed in fights.

One day in September 1893, Melanie learned that Robert had been killed in 1864, fighting mere miles from home. Locals said that Melanie was never the same following that day.

"She acted peculiarly," Jasper said. "At night, she would go outside sometimes dressed in the white gown she had made for her wedding day and walk the woods, and those who saw her said she was always talking to someone. She would usually sit around a big fire outdoors and tell her concerned relatives not to worry for she was never alone."

One November, relatives were worried when they had not seen Melanie for several days. They found her house empty, but in a basement where the woman stored the fruits and vegetables she canned during the summer, they found Melanie, dressed in her gown and hanging from a ceiling rafter. In one hand was a letter Robert had written her.

Jasper took McQuillen three doors down to talk to her nephew, Steven Hull, who became a believer after a ghostly encounter a year earlier, in mid-October 1983. Hull was driving home when he had a flat. Lacking a spare tire, he started walking to get help from his aunt.

"I noticed a young man dressed in odd-looking clothes walking above the ditch alongside of me," Hull stated. "I thought I would be neighborly, so I invited him down to walk with me, and too I wanted to know who he saw. Well, he stepped across the ditch beside me not saying a word. And when I looked into the face, I was almost paralyzed with fear, for that wasn't no man walking beside me."

Hull sprinted to Jasper's home, where she said "he came bursting into our house as white as a sheet." Hull said, "I'll never forget it as long as I live."

An even scarier episode also occurred in 1983. Some hunters were walking down a narrow path through the woods when they found a blond-haired woman sitting beside a big fire. At their approach, one of the hunters said, the woman quietly turned and looked at them.

"Her eyes were as bright as fire," the hunter said. "We knew she was a spirit of a haunt because she didn't look exactly like a human. We backed all the way back to our campsite and left in a hurry. The next day, we all went back to the same place, and there was no sign of her or evidence of a fire." It was the strangest thing any of the young men had ever witnessed.

Jasper thinks that the ghosts are those of Melanie and Robert, who were never able to meet again in life and seem unable to reunite even in the afterlife.

Fight Your Fingers to the Bone and What Do You Get?

A man who grew up in a rundown house in Paulding County related quite a tale. At age twelve, he was first alerted to a potential ghost when a man repairing the heater told him that the house was haunted. At a later date, the boy woke up with a "ghost over me, putting his hands on my face and shoulders." The apparition wore a black cape, long black gloves and an antique top hat, and "his face was just a black shadow." The lad dove under his covers and started screaming. Later that night, someone with bony fingers attempted to drag him off the bed. Years later, the boy's sister visited the Cyclorama and noticed a picture of their house hanging on a wall. A description noted that the structure had been a Civil War hospital.

A Ghostly Amputation

An Internet message board posting from "Cindy" in Theodore, Alabama, described her husband's great-grandfather, who lost the bottom half of his arm at Dallas, a failed Confederate attack that followed New Hope Church and Pickett's Mill. They successfully searched for his grave, and Cindy had her husband stand behind the tombstone for a photograph. Later, "when we got the film back, his arm was cut off by the marker in about the same form as where his ancestor had lost his!"

PART III
GRAY SPIRITS OF NORTHEAST GEORGIA

There was little military activity during the Civil War in northeast Georgia, but that does not mean there is a lack of war-related hauntings. The old arsenal grounds, now the campus of Augusta State University, have produced many spirits, as do the antebellum residences of Athens. Georgia's most important general, James Longstreet, remains in Gainesville, and one of the state's best-known political figures, Robert Toombs, hangs around Washington, where ghosts related to the fabled lost treasure of the Confederacy are common.

THE MOUNTAINS: STRANGE CIVIL WAR DETONATIONS

Some Georgia mountains are "balds," eroded on the summits to bare rock, with no vegetation. Since about 1850, mysterious noises, described by observers as the distant firing of cannons, have been heard emanating from Rabun Bald, one of Georgia's highest peaks, located in Rabun County near the North Carolina line. The distant "booms" have been heard at different points about the mountain, in all kinds of weather and throughout the year by dozens of people. Long periods of time have passed without the guns being heard, even by those who camp out on the mountain.

In November 1884, two gentlemen spent the night atop the peak. At 10:00 p.m., a series of explosive sounds was heard. They thought at first that they were the result of cannons firing at Walhalla, South Carolina, in celebration of the presidential election, "but soon the sounds were found to issue From the Ground and from a ridge to the southwest of the mountain," reported the *Monthly Weather Review* in 1897. "The explosive sounds continued till late in the night. At times they seemed to proceed from the ground immediately under the observers."

There have been numerous local theories to explain the sounds. Many thought that they were the ghostly activity of two men killed there in the 1860s, victims of bushwhackers—or perhaps the bushwhackers themselves, hunted down by militia during the Civil War. Such underground explosions, which scientists generally speculate are seismic in nature, are heard at locations around the globe.

Dahlonega

Civil War ghosts are scarce in the mountains, but a woman named Maggie passed on a story about North Georgia College in Georgia's gold city of Dahlonega. "It is rumored that the spirits of the Blue Ridge Rifle members who died during the Civil War haunt the cemetery behind one of the dorms," she wrote. "Also [there] are rumors of other strange happenings on and near campus." The Blue Ridge Rifles were organized in Dahlonega in June 1861 and fought until the end at Appomattox.

In her book *Dahlonega Haunts: Ghostly Adventures in a Georgia Mountain Town*, Amy Blackmarr had a unique format. She visited Dahlonega's haunted locales in the company of psychic Brian Keith, relying heavily on his insights.

After the fall of Atlanta in autumn 1864, Blackmarr wrote, three men—Solomon Stanberry, Iley Stuart and James Witt—stopped at a farm in Dial, Fannin County, to have their horses reshod. The Unionists were en route to Cleveland, Tennessee, where they planned to enlist in the Federal army. Unfortunately for them, they were surrounded and captured by the Confederate Home Guard, transported to Dahlonega and imprisoned upstairs in the courthouse. One night in October, four Confederates marched the three to Bearden's Bridge Hill and shot them to death.

While two men were searching for the execution site, one was suddenly struck like "a ton of bricks. The blood went out of my head and I started panicking and sweating." Court documents later confirmed the site. "I'll never forget that feeling," he said. "It was a scary experience."

One of the executioners was First Sergeant William Reese Crisson, founder of the Crisson Gold Mine, where tourists can still pan for gold. Blackmarr and Keith visited the site, where Keith felt the terror of Stanberry and Witt, believing they were "really brutalized" before being shot. Keith also found the soul of Crisson present, "traumatized by what he's done. That's why his soul doesn't rest," Keith said. Crisson is bound here, he continued. "This is his personal hell." The mine owner will endure this personal purgatory until he realizes that Jesus paid his price.

A number of Confederate veterans are buried at Mount Hope Cemetery, their graves marked annually with small flags. According to Brian Keith, all their elderly souls hang out at a building south of the Dahlonega Square, where young people were recruited as cadets of North Georgia College. A flag lay on the ground ten feet away from the grave of Nicholas Howard, a Confederate surgeon. "He threw that flag down so somebody would stop and talk," Keith declared.

GAINESVILLE

The Scapegoat Spirit

Lieutenant General James Longstreet was one of the greatest generals of the Civil War. The Confederate leader, called "[my] Old War Horse" by Robert E. Lee and known as the "Bull of the Woods" for his breakthrough assault at Chickamauga, served gallantly in most of the war's major battles. Unfortunately, after Lee's death, a conspiracy of Southern generals pinned the Confederacy's loss on Longstreet's actions at Gettysburg. The charges were ludicrous, but they still linger today.

Ostracized by Southern society, Longstreet retired to Gainesville, where he planted a vineyard and opened the Piedmont Hotel. He was often found at the local railroad station, as he traveled extensively in his later years and greeted many distinguished visitors to his establishment. After his home burned down in 1889, Longstreet lived in the Piedmont. There he entertained Daniel Sickles, U.S. congressman and Union general; Confederate general Joseph E. Johnston; writer Joel Chandler

Lieutenant General James Longstreet, known as Lee's "Old War Horse," is thought to remain in the hotel that he and his wife once ran.

Harris; newspaperman Henry Grady; and a young Woodrow and Ellen Wilson, whose second daughter, Jessie, was born here on August 28, 1887.

Longstreet died at age ninety in Gainesville and was buried at the city's Alta Vista Cemetery. Confederate officials were few in attendance, but enlisted men appreciated Longstreet's accomplishments and attended in droves.

Longstreet's last words, spoken to his second wife, were, "Helen, we shall be happier at this post." Not quite as dramatic as Stonewall Jackson's final statement, but perhaps they both had a vision of paradise. Longstreet seems to have taken his final post at the Piedmont.

"We read in old newspapers about a figure seen in the steam of locomotives at the railroad station down the street," wrote Richard Pilcher of the Longstreet Society, which works diligently to preserve the general's legacy in Gainesville. "When the steam cleared, the figure was always gone. Local residents of that day thought the wispy figure to be General Longstreet."

Constructed in 1873 as a summer resort, the U-shaped Piedmont Hotel, three stories tall, contained forty rooms with a large attached dining room and kitchen. Everyone believed that the Piedmont Hotel had been demolished in 1918, but research in 1994 revealed that a portion of it survived and had been transformed into a duplex apartment building. This remainder, the west wing's first floor, consisting of a long hall with four rooms on each side, was purchased by the Longstreet Society, which in 1997 renovated and restored it to house the Longstreet Museum.

A number of workers told stories of a supernatural presence. On a day when only two carpenters were working, one of them was inside when he heard what he presumed to be his partner walking down the hall. He spoke to the man on the other side of the wall, but at that moment, he glanced up and spotted the other carpenter outside. The first man ran outside, and they watched the doors for a while, but no one exited the building. After mustering up their nerve, they searched the house, finding no living entity.

The presence in the house moved cigarettes (Longstreet himself loved a good cigar) and tools from room to room. Closed doors were found open, and open doors were unaccountably closed. It even stole cookies from a lunchbox. Although Pilcher had experienced nothing unusual, he accepts the fact that "really serious people whom I would trust with my life have told me they feel a presence in a certain place in the hotel."

Two Longstreet Society members, Johnny and Nickiy Payne, volunteered to spend a night in the hotel and see what would happen. As soon as they entered the building, the hair on the back of Johnny's neck stood straight up. The two had just retired to their sleeping bags at 11:00 p.m. when they heard a sound from the hall: heavy boots walking down the corridor. Both jumped up to investigate but found nothing. As they settled down again, the sound was repeated. This time, they searched the entire house and the grounds but detected no evidence of an intruder.

The Paynes finally got to sleep. Hours later, Nickiy woke her husband and asked him to cover her while she used the bathroom—a portable toilet placed in an adjoining room. Awakening, Johnny asked Nickiy if she smelled what he had detected—the heavy aroma of a cigar. She did. Longstreet was apparently enjoying one of his great passions.

While Nickiy was gone, Johnny, standing in the doorway, heard someone exhaling loudly in the room behind him. Whirling around, he saw nothing. But he did smell the pungent cigar again.

The Longstreet Society sponsors tours of Longstreet's Gainesville, and an impressive monument marks his grave at Alta Vista Cemetery. On most visits, I find an empty whiskey bottle and two cigars at the grave. Maybe such an offering would placate the ghost of the Piedmont Hotel.

In this remnant of James Longstreet's hotel in Gainesville, the smell of his cigars and the sound of his heavy footsteps have been experienced.

In October 2007, my wife, Earline, and I were driving through Gainesville when I decided to check on the Piedmont Hotel. By good fortune, Richard Pilcher was working on the property. The three of us sat talking about the Piedmont when we heard a loud *whooshing* sound terminating in a muffled thud. Amused, Pilcher glanced around the room and commented, "Maybe that's the general's ghost I heard about."

Leaving the Piedmont, we discovered the cause of the disturbance we heard within. There was barely a wind, but across the street, a large branch had broken off a pecan tree and plummeted to the pavement one foot from our vehicle. We stared at it for a moment, and I said, "I guess the general was saying hello." Fortunately, I've only written nice things about him.

AUGUSTA

The Ghost that Goes to College

When the Civil War started, the Augusta Arsenal was one of Georgia's most important military facilities. During the war, the city became a major manufacturer of armaments, and the largest gunpowder factory in the world was constructed there.

Near the arsenal was the Walker House, home to a famed martial family. Its contrary Civil War patriarch was William H.T. Walker. The enemies of the United States had so riddled Walker that his nickname was "Old Shotpouch." Perhaps it was his physical condition that made him so ornery. He fought with every superior and had challenged his corps commander, Major General William Hardee, to a duel minutes before leading his men into the Battle of Atlanta. He was dead before combat began, shot by a Union picket. (The spot is marked by an upended cannon at I-20, Exit 30, Glenwood Avenue in Atlanta.) By the time his body reached Augusta for burial, it had traveled across much of Georgia to avoid Federal forces. Upon arrival, his sword was missing. Maybe the general remains pissed off at the imagined slights during life, or perhaps he is still searching for his blade.

The Augusta Arsenal was shut down in 1955, but its buildings and the Walker House, with its family cemetery, were incorporated into the campus of Augusta College, now Regents State University.

Enter Dr. Keith Cowling, a cultured professor of English and a native of Great Britain, who arrived in Augusta in the late 1950s. After working late one night in the Fine Arts Building, Dr. Cowling left his office at 8:15 p.m. and walked to the parking lot. He was cranking his car when he spotted a lone figure strolling across campus. Because the school had recently suffered a number of thefts, Cowling kept an eye on the shadowy person.

The man was dressed in what resembled an old-fashioned "gray English-style overcoat and a yellow scarf was tied around his waist," wrote Nancy Roberts, who interviewed Cowling for *Georgia Ghosts*. "His hat had its brim turned up on one side in that carefree, dashing manner" of Australians, Cowling noted. The "unusual fashion" led him to think that the man was returning "props to the drama department."

The man in gray crossed a road and passed the Fine Arts Building, apparently heading for the entrance to the Walker Cemetery. Cowling put the car in drive and slowly followed the mysterious figure, who was oblivious to the professor's presence. At the entrance to the cemetery, "he seemed to vanish," probably behind a tree, the educator believed. However, "I was left with the feeling that the whole thing was very odd," he believed. "The more I thought about it on my way home, the more strange the incident seemed." Cowling called a friend and revealed, "I have just seen a ghost."

In the morning, the incident still occupied his mind. Cowling dismissed class early and walked over to the cemetery. The first thing he noticed was a patch of ground freshly sewn with grass seed and protected by a large strand of wire secured between two trees at waist level. A physical being would have had to duck under the obstacle or climb over it, but the figure from the previous evening had done neither. "Without a break in his stride, the figure had passed right through the wire," Cowling declared. He also noted no trees near the entrance to the cemetery and concluded that the phantom "could not have disappeared behind a tree." Also, the cemetery gate was securely locked, and the plot was surrounded by a ten-foot-high fence, "impossible to scale without a ladder."

Cowling did some historical research and decided that "the man's outfit resembled a Civil War officer's uniform." He also considered the activities that would "have surrounded the arsenal during the Civil War, with Confederate officers constantly coming and going…My excitement mounting, I recalled another point. In *Gone with the Wind*, Scarlett makes a yellow scarf to give to Ashley for the Christmas present—just the sort of scarf the young man had tied around his waist! What a figure he cut in his gray uniform, with his jaunty hat and the ends of the yellow scarf fluttering the evening breeze. I was convinced then that I had seen the ghost of a Confederate officer."

A long-deceased Confederate officer was observed walking across the Georgia Regents University campus to his grave in this cemetery.

Kathy Schofe, direction of public relations, said that the school has "about five or six ghosts." She believes that the previous story is false and likewise disparages a tale that a drummer boy haunts the graveyard. "Nope, no little drummer boy," Schofe said, "but we've got others."

While this is one specific story of a professor trailing the Confederate officer on his nighttime stroll back to the grave, it is claimed that all manner of college denizens—professors, students, administrators and custodians—have seen the officer's straight path to the gate and his physical passage through that barrier.

Dr. Ed Cashin, who once taught history at Augusta College and is author of *General Sherman's Girlfriend and Other Stories About Augusta*, said that the cemetery "invites ghosts." Also, another former professor, Dr. Helen Callahan, and a friend encountered a cold spot on a stroll through the cemetery, which contains at least seventy-four remains—forty-eight soldiers and twenty-two civilian dependents.

Rains Hall, constructed in 1827 and named for Confederate commandant Colonel George Washington Rains, served as officers' quarters at the Augusta Arsenal. It suffered severe damage in 1886 when a major earthquake ravaged Charleston, South Carolina, requiring extensive repairs. More than a century later, in 2004, additional reconstruction revealed liquor bottles, broken china and a mystery. Behind the walls, a worker found a beautiful pair of bathing slippers, hand-woven of hemp or another natural fiber and decorated with pink and green circles. Archaeologists dated the style to the 1870s or 1880s, so they were apparently inserted during earthquake restoration, probably out of superstition.

"The idea is that they are supposed to avert some kind of evil disaster coming into the residence and harming the residents," stated Chris Murphy. The practice is documented in Great Britain, other European counties and the United States, where they were commonly placed near doors, windows or chimneys.

Augusta State University, recently renamed Georgia Regents University, has embraced its spirited residents. Near Halloween in 2004, seven employees spent their lunch in the president's garden, relating their personal tales of the paranormal to seventy-five students and staffers, the occasion recorded by Greg Rickabugh of the *Augusta Chronicle*. President William Bloodworth appeared with a can of "ghost repellent," guaranteed to prevent "most common household hauntings," he joked. He intended to "spray myself several times over the next couple of days."

When the slippers were removed from Rains Hall, where his office and the public relations department are located, Bloodworth joked about replacing them to ensure good fortune. Physical Plant director Therese Rosier, known for her collection of footwear, donated a pair of gold sequined pumps, which were sealed within the walls. "Why take any chances?" Bloodworth said. "I wouldn't say I'm superstitious, but I wouldn't be the first to say there's nothing to these paranormal experiences."

Public relations director Kathy Schofe witnessed paranormal events in Rains Hall for ten years. Working after hours with another employee one evening, they heard doorknobs being rattled throughout the building. They hoped that it was security checking the premises, but no guards ever appeared.

"We grabbed our purses, got midway down the stairs and then heard a conversation in the basement," Schofe told Kimberly Lawson. "It was like a radio turned down low in the car; you really couldn't make out what they were saying. We turned right back around and called public safety so we could be escorted to our cars."

Another coworker, Kim Smith, was also in Rains when she heard a strange noise in the hall. "I ran out, and all the blinds on the windows were fluttering, as if someone was running their hand down them. There was no breeze, and none of the windows were open."

Footsteps are heard in empty halls, and cigarette smoke is detected in the smoke-free building. Security personnel regularly stop by as lights are mysteriously turned on in the locked building at night. Many witnesses call the spirit "George" or "Colonel." At different times, the *Augusta Chronicle* and the *Bell Ringer* (the newspaper of the school) have reported employees' accounts of a Confederate soldier standing on the staircase in the building. A custodian has seen a figure clad in a cavalry hat and flared pants, which indicates an era later than the Civil War.

Boykin Wright Hall (1900) was constructed opposite the cemetery by its namesake, a Georgia Supreme Court judge. The building, which Boykin's daughter donated to Augusta University, might or might not retain the spirit of Wright.

One Friday, employee Cyndi White was speaking to colleague Gina Thurman when a noise was heard from above. Although they knew that no one was upstairs, they still feared that "someone had fell down, as if they fell and rolled." Investigating, the only thing amiss was a light plastic frame that had fallen to the floor. "There was no way that little picture frame

Boykin-Wright Hall, a former U.S. Arsenal building now part of Georgia Regents University, is thoroughly haunted by its namesake.

could have made that loud of a noise," White told *Augusta* magazine, "so we thought it had to be the ghost."

On Monday, three days later, Gina and Cyndi were talking with a student near the front door of the building when they all observed a dark figure, visible from its head to shoulder, through a glass portion of the entrance. "A gray shadow, a silhouette of a person, appeared at the door, got closer and then faded into nothing," Thurman told Kimberly Lawson. The student even moved aside when she heard the door handle being jiggled, but no one was there.

"Cyndi and I saw this image in the window, and you could tell it was a person," Gina said, "but you couldn't make out facial features. It was black, but you could see through it. As it moved, it got light and lighter until it disappeared. We were kind of convinced that it was him." Added White, "I didn't believe in ghosts until that happened."

Boykin is considered a friendly ghost, his presence announced by rattling doorknobs and a feeling of comfort, and he enters through the front door and walks down the hall, sometimes as a dark figure, other times transparent, wearing clothing from the 1800s. He usually disappears at the end of his jaunt but has been seen sitting behind a desk. These personal appearances are "very peaceful," White stated, and often occur in March.

One room in Boykin Hall remained locked for years, the key long missing. When the room was finally entered, it was discovered that the door had been secured with a dead bolt lock from the *inside*.

"There have been people in the building by themselves," Ginny Luke, a long-term worker, told the *Augusta Metro Spirit* on October 23, 2002, "and they've heard two people arguing." That ghost, dubbed "Emily," enjoys playing with the telephone system and watching television. "It just pops on," Luke said. "One day, she was watching *The Today Show*. We like her as a friendly ghost."

Bloody Mary

The Benét House, home to commandants of the Augusta Arsenal, was named for one: Colonel J. Walker Benét, who served from 1911 to 1919. His children, Stephen Vincent and William Rose, both won Pulitzer Prizes for poetry.

One story at Benét House involves a wife whose husband was usually hunting if not attending to arsenal business. She spent her time shopping and admiring her extensive wardrobe, where, appropriately enough, she was found dead one day. Everyone agreed that the husband had poisoned her, but in that pre-*CSI* world, evidence was lacking. The Clothes Horse Ghost manifests itself in mirrors, still admiring her dresses, and has been seen by many students and administrators. Brenda Johnson, a nineteen-year veteran of the office of admissions, glimpsed things in a mirror. "It's like a gray flash, and then it's gone," she said. She described the incidents as eerie, and at night, she had heard phantom footsteps. "I don't like coming in here by myself," she confided. A legend she related described a rocking chair heard in motion somewhere in the old house.

The wife's spirit also occasionally revisits the closet. Johnson was working one night with a colleague when their attention was drawn to a noise emanating from upstairs. The sounds led them to the closet, where hangers were being bashed together by unseen hands. "She's up there," Johnson believed. "She's angry about the fact that other women have moved in." Several years earlier, construction workers saw someone in the building at night when the structure was deserted, but their search revealed no one.

A post–Civil War ghost story involves an arsenal employee of the northern persuasion. The man employed his incompetent nephew and paid him a higher salary than other workers, making the nephew the target of their ire. Upon entering the house one day, the delicious aroma of a freshly baked apple pie drew him upstairs, where he was dispatched by a pistol bullet. His body was interred at Walker Cemetery, but his spirit, naturally known as the Apple Pie Ghost, remains. Occasionally, when the scent of apple pie wafts throughout the structure, his footsteps are heard traversing the stairs. The young man is also heard opening and shutting exterior doors, the oven and cupboards, forever seeking dessert. People frequently believe they are being watched or followed through the halls.

Another employee, Ben Atkins, assistant to the admissions director, heard doors open and shut themselves at night. A rocking chair creaked, and footsteps were heard upstairs. Objects that rearranged themselves in the building might be the work of what Atkins called "our resident poltergeist," which he attempted to mollify. "I talk to it when I arrive, and I talk to it when I leave," he admitted, an approach taken by others in similar situations. Treating ghosts like they are a part of one's everyday life often seems to help.

I See Nothing

Carolyn Giles worked in the Benét House. When she was there alone on Saturday, she notified campus security…just in case. "And I turn my radio on because I know this is supposed to be a haunted building, and I don't want to see or hear anything while I am in there by myself." She has glimpsed objects "flashing through the hallway." Her only reaction was to turn the radio up with the hope that whatever it was would leave her unmolested.

Joyce A. Jones, dean of students, believed that the ghosts were just reminding them of the school's history. "They don't want us to forget them," Joyce said.

Payne Hall is named for Captain Matthew Payne, who was responsible for much of the arsenal. The three-story structure was a storage unit for many of the weapons and other equipment that an army needs. Beneath the basement, according to Scott Johnson, was a small subbasement where prisoners were kept and supposedly taken out for execution. Used as headquarters for the arsenal when it closed in 1955, Augusta State University renovated it for school usage. The cell area was closed, and the location of its entrance was lost to history. Now housing the Academic Affairs, Financial Aid, Registrar, Veterans Affairs and Academic and Architectural Planning Offices, employees and students who ventured to the basement were often overwhelmed by extreme feelings of claustrophobia. Many refused to return to the subterranean lair of condemned soldiers past.

One construction worker said that "he wasn't going back in there at night anymore," said Dr. Robert Mays, Augusta's director of counseling and testing. "There were too many strange things. Doors opening and shutting."

Columbia County

The Arbor Day Ghost

In the mid-1800s, a planter named Benjamin Bragg purchased 696 acres in Columbia County near Martinez. He constructed a home known as Cedar Grove due to the forest of trees he planted in front of the house on the barren land. Bragg died during the conflict, apparently not of war-related causes, and years later, his wife, Frances, married again, making a fine match with George Washington Evans Jr. They had met during the war when Frances and other women gathered in Augusta to sew Confederate uniforms. Evans, a widower with eleven children, was a former mayor of Augusta and quartermaster and chief of the Georgia Clothing Bureau.

Evans never owned the land, and Frances required him to sign a prenup—if she died first, her children, and not the general, would inherit the land. Evans died in 1876, aged seventy-two, and is buried at Magnolia Cemetery in Augusta. The family sold the property in 1903, and it was owned by a succession of families. Eventually, the house and seven acres were donated to the Episcopal Diocese of Georgia and now belongs to the Church of Our Savior, serving as the parish house, located behind the church near the junction of Columbia Road and Washington Road. Rooms were used as classrooms and for other church activities.

Three priests (two of whom refused to stay in the structure after dark) and a number of parishioners have reported seeing lights moving from room to room when the structure was unoccupied, and some have heard a man in hobnailed boots walking about the house. Father Harry Thompson said that the ghostly manifestations did not start until thirty-two cedar trees were cut down during construction of a new church. Phantom voices, occasionally constituting entire conversations, have been heard from empty rooms, the talk sometimes accompanied by footfalls. One day, the door to a supply closet was opened, and according to Scott A. Johnson in *The Mayor's Guide: The Stately Ghosts of Augusta*, "the products began flying off the shelves, smashing into the wall behind him." It seems that Bragg or Evans has returned to express displeasure with alterations to the property. There is also a belief that Frances murdered Evans by poisoning and that this is why his spirit lingers. Another explanation was suggested when excavation on the grounds revealed bones—the structure may have been built atop a Native American or early settler graveyard. The house is still used by the Church of Our Savoir.

Part of the Cedar Grove plantation was developed into the Holiday Park Subdivision. Former resident Dr. Gerald J. Smith, an English professor, stated that some "spooky" activity was always occurring while he lived there. "You could actually hear what sounded like conversations going on in the house, and there was nobody in the house except me or somebody else. I was always hearing some kind of noise going on. It was a common occurrence." He believes that these supernatural phenomena occurred because the housing development covered the graves of slaves. He doesn't believe that the events occurred because of the cedar trees. "I think it's because the slaves' sprits were disturbed."

Washington

Ghostly Gold Guards

I think of Washington, Georgia, as the end of the Civil War. Fugitive Jefferson Davis disbanded his cabinet here, and it was the entry point of many ragged, emaciated soldiers returning from Virginia and North Carolina. It was also the scene of one of the great mysteries of the Civil War. Many writers have mangled the story of the lost treasure of the Confederacy. In brief, as Richmond was evacuated, a train carrying Davis and other prominent officials was packed with the remaining treasury of the CSA and the assets from the city's banks. Much of these treasures are accounted for, but some portion disappeared, and according to what theory you endorse, it is secreted somewhere between northeast Georgia and northern Florida.

Enter the story of Michael Horgan, longtime caretaker of the Callaway Plantation, a complex of historic structures on the outskirts of Washington, as recorded in Nancy Roberts's *Georgia Ghosts*. He occupied a mobile home on the premises after graduating from the University of Georgia Law School in the mid-1980s.

One night, after a double date, a friend named Jack stayed with Horgan. Near daybreak, they were awakened by Michael's dogs, which were running around barking at something behind the Callaway house. "I don't think I've ever heard them barking like that before," Horgan said as he pocketed a pistol. The men quietly investigated, and as they stepped around the corner of the house, they came face to face with four mounted men in worn Confederate uniforms.

"The riders stared at us, and we stared back," Michael said, "but not a word was spoken. Then they reined in their horses, turned away from us and rode off in the direction of Washington. The dogs were crazy barking, but they made no move to follow." After the horsemen disappeared into the misty darkness, the men realized that the troopers, their horses and their equipment had not emitted a single sound.

Michael took the positive track, thinking that they were part of the guard for the Confederate gold, while Jack suggested that they might have been looking to steal some. Horgan rejects a belief in ghosts but admitted, "When I hear the dogs bark at night, I always think about those four horsemen."

Robert Toombs and the Dissolution of the Union

Georgia has seen few figures as controversial as Robert Toombs (1810–1885), a major character of the turbulent mid-nineteenth century. One of the most influential citizens in Georgia history, Toombs served in Georgia's House of Representatives, the United States House of Representatives and Senate and as a general and secretary of state for the Confederacy. He was also a successful lawyer and planter.

Perhaps the weirdest story has Toombs breakfasting in Washington, D.C., with fellow senator John C. Calhoun in 1850. Calhoun, a prominent advocate of secession, was a militant war hawk and fire-eater. The former vice president's appearance at breakfast was so haggard that Toombs expressed concern for his health.

Calhoun proceeded to tell a strange tale. The previous evening, as he sat in his room writing, a confident stranger, his face concealed by a cloak, appeared and took a seat. The phantom asked what Calhoun was writing. It was a document of secession, Calhoun replied. The menacing vision then asked for Calhoun's right hand. As the stranger arose, the cloak fell away, and his true character was revealed. It was a spectral George Washington, clad in his military uniform. The apparition grasped Calhoun's hand and asked if he would use the paper to dissolve the Union. When Calhoun affirmed that he would if necessary, a black spot suddenly appeared on the back of his hand. Washington then declared that a similar sign marked Benedict Arnold "in the next world." Calhoun then awoke and found the black spot still on the back of his right hand, which he showed Toombs. Calhoun died within the year. I personally do not give much credence to this story, primarily because I have been unable to locate its original source.

Toombs's home is located in the wonderfully preserved town of Washington in Wilkes County, abutting the South Carolina line. His classic Greek Revival mansion (Toombs opposed a hotel for the community, stating that any respectable visitor could stay with him and that Washington should not host any disreputable traveler), constructed in 1794, was obtained by the State of Georgia forty years ago.

"Since the late 1970s when the house was first restored," noted a website sponsored by the Georgia State Parks and Historic Sites, "many eerie encounters have been reported. Some of the current staff has reported no incidents, but a list of ghostly occurrences from the past is kept on file in the office."

"On many occasions, the Site Managers and other personnel have heard and seen doorknobs turning with no one behind the door, and outside doors closing with no one around the area inside or outside," the site record continues. "Also, during restoration a carpenter was working on the second floor stairway that leads to the top floor, when he heard noises coming from the Toombs bedroom. He came downstairs to find out if anyone else was in the house and the curator said no. He went back upstairs and resumed his work only to hear the noises again. Eventually, he left and another carpenter had to come in to finish the work." The persistent tapping sounds could never be explained, but that is the room where Toombs died in 1885.

Several workers have reported an otherworldly figure they refer to as the "Lady in White," who is sometimes accompanied by a "Gentleman in a Brown Suit." When a curator started to climb the stairs to the top floor, "she looked up and saw the 'Lady in White,'" the record states. "The curator went downstairs to the museum and never went upstairs alone again." The ghostly couple has been seen frequently on the stair steps and landings,

The Washington home of Robert Toombs, U.S. senator and Confederate general, whose ghostly presence is detected here and at the University of Georgia.

exiting the Ladies Parlor and entering a second-floor hallway. The woman is thought to be Toombs's great-niece, Miss Kathleen Colley, whose mother, Mrs. Fred Colley, inherited the residence in 1888. A visitor who frequented the house as a child when his mother visited the Colleys never saw the woman wearing any other color, and in archived photographs, "it's true she always has on white," the state maintains. The man is assumed to be Toombs. At the Georgia historic park, the state website stated, "exhibits and displays are not the only things visitors might catch sight of while touring."

"We see the lady over and over," said Marcia Campbell, curator of the Toombs House. "But she doesn't seem to be aware of our presence." "There's definitely something going on here. I've seen them, and too many other people have reported seeing things and hearing things, to deny it. I don't want to appear to have a haunted house here, but…"

On my last visit to the Toombs House, employees were tight-lipped about the topic of ghosts.

Elbert County

The legend of the lost treasure of the Confederacy spills over into Elbert County, according to Robin Segars and Anne Wilson. They tell of the Allen House (the county's oldest), constructed in 1783 and built by Beverly Allen. The owner acknowledged that the place is haunted but insisted that she has never seen a ghost. However, there were other incidents. An antique Seth Thomas clock rested on a mantel in the dining room. It had not been wound for fifteen years when a granddaughter was to be married in the sunken gardens on the grounds on July 10 at 10:30 a.m. Several months before the event, the hands started moving with no external motivation. The hands moved faster and faster on July 10, and exactly at 10:30 a.m., they reached the 10:30 a.m. spot on the clock face and then stopped. The clock seemed content to have helped in the celebration, but several months later, the hands started moving again. They stopped at the exact moment that a family member died. To date, the clock has not started itself up again.

There is also an old square piano in the parlor of the Allen House. On a number of occasions, the owner has heard music while occupying the room, but when she attempted to listen to the tune, it immediately ceased. One night, she awakened to a sound "like someone running his hands through a pan of dishwater."

Workers reported a number of supernatural events on the grounds but insisted that only those gifted with the second sight can actually view a ghost. There are also stories that $50,000 of the Confederate treasure is secreted somewhere on the old plantation.

Gwinnett County

In another haunting out of time, a Union soldier appeared in a modern housing development in 1985, at the Ridgewood Subdivision in Gwinnett County. Two children of one house, according to their mother, sighted a man wearing a blue uniform and a hat featuring a star at different times, once on a staircase and another in a bedroom. A visiting nephew saw the figure appear in the kitchen and later in his bedroom. The young man refused to spend another night in the house.

Athens: Civil War Ghosts of the Classic City

Because Federal raiders were turned away in July 1864, no battles were fought in Athens. However, this antebellum city was a cultural, educational and political center of Georgia, providing a number of Confederate leaders to the cause, particularly Cobb brothers Howell and T.R.R., both noted generals. Their houses are reported as haunted, but ironically, only the house of a third Cobb brother, John, hosts a Confederate spirit.

T.R.R. Cobb Hasn't Been Resurrected Yet, But His House Has

Thomas Reade Rootes Cobb was an early Georgia leader in law, education, politics and the military. He was the reporter for the Georgia Supreme Court (his father-in-law, Henry Lumpkin, was Georgia's first state chief justice), codified Georgia's laws, turned Franklin College into the University of Georgia while founding the school's law school and established the Lucy

The Athens grave of Thomas R.R. Cobb, Confederate general and legal expert, whose essence remains in his former home.

Cobb Institute in Athens for women. A secessionist firebrand, he attended the Georgia State Convention in 1860 and wrote a new state constitution a year later. As a member of the Confederate Provisional Congress, he was the primary author of the Confederate Constitution. Fitting action to words, he organized Cobb's Legion and became its colonel in Virginia, rising to the rank of brigadier general and fighting well at Antietam. Three months later, on December 13, 1862, as he defended the fabled stone wall at Fredericksburg, Cobb was mortally wounded by an exploding artillery shell and died within sight of the house in which he had been born.

The T.R.R. Cobb House (1830) in Athens was a wedding present for Cobb and his wife, Marion. In the 1850s, they added octagonal wings and a grand Greek Revival portico. When threatened with demolition in 1984, the house was moved to Stone Mountain Park to await restoration funds that never came. Twenty years later, the house was returned to Athens, several blocks from its original location, and restored by the Watson-Brown Foundation. It opened for tours in August 2007, emphasizing the history of the house and its former owners, and it hosts conferences about nineteenth-century southern life.

Traditionally, the T.R.R. Cobb House sports the wraith of a man clad in a colorful dressing gown that has often been observed descending the stairs and entering a drawing room, where he sits beside the fire. It could very well be that Cobb has returned from the hell of combat to relax in his beloved earthly home.

The house was once owned by St. Stephens Catholic Church, which was adjacent to the house, and served as a rectory. Since the Cobb House opened, a staff member of the house said, "Two priests have come to visit us. Both, independently of each other, asked us if we knew about the ghost. We had all heard some strange sounds in the house, but we had not actually seen an apparition. What they described to us was a man in gray who would descend the staircase and walk into the library in the octagon on Mr. Cobb's side of the house, where he would stand in front of the fireplace."

The priests also believed that a supernatural force was keeping watch over the building. "They told us that while they were using the house," the worker continued, "they had gotten into the bad habit of stacking their newspapers on one of the outside porches, and there were newspapers stacked from floor to ceiling right beside the house. One day, the papers caught on fire, and every newspaper was burned to cinders, yet none of the fire touched the house at all. They said that something was certainly protecting the house. They assured us that the ghost they had seen was completely benevolent, and we believe that it must be T.R.R. Cobb."

While working in the house, the employee and others have heard various unexplainable sounds. "We do hear footsteps downstairs in the house, most of the time when it is just I or the curator in the house. I've also heard a little girl laughing downstairs. Each time we hear these things, we come down, thinking someone is here, having come through the front door and we didn't hear them, and there will be no one here. No one at all."

The Cobbs lost three children in the house, two infant sons and a daughter named Lucy. "I like to think that the little girl I heard laughing downstairs was probably Lucy," the staff member said, "because it did seem to come from the room where her portrait is.

"We have T.R.R. Cobb's armoire sitting at the base of the stairs, and every now and then, we'll come down and the doors will be open. We'll close them and we'll come back down later, and the doors will be open once more. The funny thing is, when we're giving a tour and we want to open the doors, often it has been difficult to do. It doesn't seem incredibly likely that those doors would open on their own."

The beautifully restored Athens home of T.R.R. Cobb. The general is reluctant to vacate.

The same phenomenon occurs with a piece of furniture, called a secretary, in Cobb's sitting room. "Every now and then, those doors will open and we'll try to shut them, and they will not stay closed. We think that maybe Cobb's looking for something. Once, I heard someone knocking on the sidelights by the front door and came downstairs thinking someone wanted to get in. Not only was there no one there, but the front door was standing wide open. I looked around to see if anyone was walking away from the house, but there was no one in sight."

The employee explained that no one "has ever felt anything at all sinister. We do not feel one bit uncomfortable about it because whatever it is seems very happy with what we're doing here. We can't explain these things, but they happen from time to time."

Brother Cobb

In historical circles, T.R.R. Cobb is usually the "other" Cobb, but in the paranormal world, brother Howell Cobb is. Howell fought well at

Crampton's Gap, Maryland, before returning home to Georgia to command Georgia governor Joseph Brown's militia. His house on Pope Street is said to be haunted by the ghost of Mary Thomas Safford, who committed suicide during postpartum depression. The sound of blood dripping from the balcony where she offed herself can be heard, but only when an infant is present in the house.

Ghostis Interruptus

The John B. Cobb House, divided into several separate residences in the 1960s, once hosted three different ghosts. The primary occurrence surrounds the marriage in the house of Jefferson Lamar to Mary, a stepdaughter of the Cobbs, on July 22, 1861. The story claims that the couple danced before Lamar left immediately to join Howell Cobb's unit in Virginia, even before the marriage was consummated. Lamar disappeared at Crampton's Gap in September 1862, presumably killed in the battle there that preceded the great clash at Antietam Creek a few days later. Lamar's death was allegedly announced in the house by the ghost of a long-deceased family nursemaid. Susan Frances Barrow Tate heard many stories of the cursed couple, together again in the afterlife, dancing in the parlor, until the house was dismembered.

Another story had the newly installed gaslights going out the night of the wedding. Candles were laid out while hasty repairs were made to the system. Thereafter, whenever the house experienced lighting problems, ghostly figures were seen attempting to help illuminate the home.

Dr. Frances Scott purchased the oldest part of the Cobb House and moved it, appropriately enough, to Cobb Street. Mary B. Warren said that Dr. Scott was "not one to give over to such things," but she confided that on several occasions her dog barked at an invisible presence on a landing. On multiple occasions, she felt like she was being watched, the experience leading her to believe in the ghost nurse.

The Lustrat House, originally home of the university's chancellor and now office of the school's president, is thought to be haunted by Dr. Charles Morris, once head of the English department and a Confederate major. Dozens of witnesses have reported sighting a man in a flowered dressing gown (or a Confederate uniform) descend the stairs from the second floor and sit in a rocking chair near the fireplace in the front dining room, much like the ghost at the T.R.R. Cobb House. Marie Lustrat and others have seen the ghost seated at a desk in front of a window in the room. After the fireplaces were bricked up during remodeling in the early 1970s, the mysterious manifestations diminished and have apparently stopped. There have been no recent sightings of Dr. Morris, who surely misses his fireside visits.

Party Ghosts

The Taylor-Grady House has two regular ghostly visitors for Christmas. A number of people have seen a ghost clad in a Confederate uniform and his gentle lady during the holidays. The house is now headquarters for the Junior League of Athens and hosts many weddings and parties. After preparing for an event late on the evening of November 30, 1991, Lynn Yarbrough and two colleagues decided to leave. At that point, they smelled liquor and felt ghostly presences. "We could just feel them all around," Yarbrough said. "It felt like someone was hovering." The trio ran from the house. Of the experience, Yarbrough said, "I just don't go there by myself anymore," a pledge made by many who have experienced the paranormal.

Toombs Goes to College

The fiery Robert Toombs had been ejected from Franklin College (now the University of Georgia) in 1828 for riotous behavior. Legend has him returning at commencement and speaking so eloquently beneath an oak tree between Demosthenian Hall and the chapel that the graduation ceremonies in the chapel were vacated as all gathered to hear Toombs's oration.

Legend further states that at the moment of his death one stormy night in 1885, the magnificent tree called "Toombs' Oak" was struck by lightning. The dead tree toppled in 1908 and was cut up and fashioned into highly prized sacred relics for UGA alums. Visit the marker, erected by the state in 1985 where the tree stood, for a traditional dose of good luck.

The validity of these two stories is open to question. One Clarke County historian maintains that Henry W. Grady, the famed Georgia newsman, invented the entire affair.

The ghost of T.R.R. Cobb has been seen to stroll into his old office in Athens.

Bad Robert! Bad!

Demosthenian Hall, a Federal-style structure located on Old Campus, the earliest part of the university, was constructed in 1824, making it the fourth-oldest building on campus. It houses the Demosthenian Literary Society, founded in 1803 and named for a famous Greek statesman and orator. To this day, the society promotes public speaking and debate. It was one of Toombs's favorite institutions on campus. Legend has a Confederate officer clad in gray, perhaps Toombs himself, haunting the building, his ghostly presence including footsteps heard in empty second-floor halls, doors opening and lampshades spinning by themselves and cold spots.

Carl Pyrdum, a member of the DLS, told William Bender in *Haunted Atlanta and Beyond*, "I have felt when I was studying really late, this sense of someone telling me to 'get out' and I've left, but I've heard other members say when they've gotten that feeling, they've told Bobby, 'No!' and the feeling went away."

Bender, a professor at UGA, explained that Toombs's continued presence on campus is not an unnatural act. "Consciousness can be independent of the human body," he stated. "Ghosts often appear in places that were important to them in life."

"Most of the members have heard footsteps when no one else was around and have heard a voice giving a speech late at night," said Kayte Servidio, a member of the society. "There was one time when one of the lights in the hall wouldn't turn off for three days, even when you flicked the switch several times. After the third day, I asked politely for the light to turn off, and it did—by itself."

The society regularly honors Toombs's memory, said Servidio. "We keep portraits of him around the hall, and we tour his family home every year"—as does Toombs himself, reportedly.

On a Lighter Note

Those clever minds at the University of Georgia compiled the "Top Ten Weird Sights of Athens, Georgia." According to that list, number seven was Phi Kappa Hall. "This was used by occupying Union troops as a stable during the Civil War," notes the list's website. "Also, according to legend, the upstairs was used as a brothel. And, on moonlit nights, you can still hear the ghostly moans of…oh, never mind!"

The Thing in the Attic

According to Internet poster "Itianitaboricua," an antebellum house near Athens saw service as a Confederate hospital. Two boys who later lived there located a hidden door leading from the kitchen up to the attic, where they found old rags that appeared to be bloodstained. After the secret door was opened, one boy awoke at night unable to move and with the certainty that a spirit was in the room with him. The paralysis lasted fifteen minutes. The same lad was climbing the stairs to his room one night and found a man, dressed in a Civil War uniform, standing on the landing. "I want to go home," the spirit said with a distant voice. The child summoned the nerve to reply, "Well, go home!" and it vanished. A heavy door to the living room would be securely locked, "but, by morning, it would be open once again."

Another legend of the house, less reputable, involves a lost Civil War treasure. During the war, residents of the house heard approaching enemy cavalry and hurriedly buried their valuables. The "cavalry" soon arrived, but it consisted of a herd of vagrant cattle. When the inhabitants went to retrieve their goods, the treasure was gone. The area has been excavated on a number of occasions, even utilizing bulldozers, but nothing has been found. This story is probably a corruption of the legendary Confederate treasure that some believe is still hidden in northeastern Georgia.

WATKINSVILLE

Watkinsville, the seat of Oconee County, preserves one of Georgia's oldest structures, the Eagle Tavern. Constructed in 1789 as an inn and tavern that doubled as a frontier fort for protection against Indian attack, it was built with rough-hewn timbers. The basement is still bare earth and stone.

Currently a welcome center, workers there believe that five to six different ghosts haunt the structure, each with their own personal space. On the first floor is a large fireplace, and one spirit seems to stick close to the chimney, according to several different psychics, and that area often exhibits a cold spot. Visitors also report a scratching sound from that locale. According to tradition, when a Union cavalry raid passed through Watkinsville on its way to Athens, where it was repulsed, a Confederate soldier hid in a loft behind the chimney.

A female employee can sense the presence of spirits in the Eagle Tavern. She does not like some, but the man on the first floor does not disturb her. "A white man, young; maybe a soldier at some point. He doesn't seem lonely and he's not bothersome," an employee named Janie told William Bender for *Haunted Atlanta and Beyond*.

WARRENTON

Mac Leathers purchased an old house in Oglethorpe County that had belonged to a Confederate officer, Second Lieutenant Pilcher. Everything was fine until Leathers decided to move the structure to Warrenton without Pilcher's beloved trunk. At the new location, windows were frequently raised and lowered by invisible means. Leathers witnessed this phenomenon at least seven times, and on occasion he felt a chill and broke out in goose bumps. Leathers quieted the spirit by fetching Pilcher's possessions and returning them to the house. "Everything stopped as soon as I brought his trunk to the house," he stated.

CONCLUSION

Although it is not worth much, people often ask what I think of these phenomena. My personal belief is that the actual souls of Civil War personalities are not being experienced. However, I do believe that the wide range of weirdness experienced at Civil War sites emanate from some unexplainable source—check out the "Miles Unified Theory of Weirdness" in the conclusion of *Weird Georgia* (2000). I would suggest that observing these phenomena is adequate excitement, but do not attempt to interact with or understand it—it can't be comprehended by mortal minds.

A Jim Miles Disclaimer

Is every story contained in this book true? Of course not! I have expressed my doubts about a few tales, and no doubt some folks concocted convincing stories that deceived me; I was possibly willingly fooled by others. Like you, I love a good story, and sometimes it is true that you can't let the facts stand in the way of a good tale. I mean, come on folks—it is a book about ghosts.

I borrowed from hundreds of sources—books, magazines, newspapers, Internet articles, tourist brochures, Georgia Department of Natural Resources press releases and tour guides (although, ironically enough, not one single ghost tour operator—I do have *some* standards), as well as all kinds of people, including a few who actually witnessed ghostly phenomena. I have also attributed sources so that you might peruse the original story. Enjoy the book. Tell the stories. Help me sell more copies of the book—my grandsons, Xavier and Emmett, need orthodontic work. Just please don't take yourself or any phenomena too seriously.

I have great faith in the veracity of those whose stories are told here. It is my long experience that those who witness and share paranormal phenomenon are decent, honest, reliable folks who relate true accounts of their experiences. I know from personal experience that, as Dickey Lee sang in 1965, strange things happen in this world (Laurie), and nobody, in my humble opinion, can adequately explain them.

The Civil War history contained in this book is true (if you think you might actually like Civil War history without ghosts, check out my more serious Civil War books). Conduct yourselves properly while seeking paranormal experiences. The American soldiers who fought and died on these battlefields deserve our respect. Cemeteries are sacred. I sincerely believe that a sighting is more likely to occur to the reverent, and I hope that a specter will send those who are disrespectful into a psychic purgatory. Do not ruin an interesting and largely harmless obsession for many by whipping up a séance and attempting to contact the spirits of great-great-grandfather Zebedee Palmer.

A Word to the Wise

Okay, actually, I meant to call this section "A Word to the Foolish" (if not the downright stupid), but Mama tried to raise me to be polite and was half-successful. Don't trespass, particularly in dark, dangerous, decrepit structures that may be occupied by the living (the dead aren't usually armed or deranged), who, if you're lucky, won't call the authorities. Don't venture onto rural properties, which are probably protected by shotguns and feral ferrets.

Make certain that you have clear advance permission from historic site managers or property owners, preferably in writing, before starting an expedition. Be careful to have with you the name, title and telephone numbers of those who have approved your operation.

If you have to ghost-hunt, find a responsible group that follows a standardized code of conduct and obey the rules. The buddy system we used when swimming at summer camp works (if it didn't, that might explain all those creepy camp legends that kept us awake in tents or cabins all night), and it is still a good idea. Never hunt alone and let a responsible party (i.e., someone smart enough to not hunt ghosts) know the particulars of your expedition.

Don't annoy the dead—their reaction to that sort of thing can be unpredictable and will likely scare the pee out of you or eat at your brains. Don't annoy the living. Don't carry firearms (except when hunting Bigfoot—those mothers are *big!*). Take your crosses and other religious artifacts with you. While I personally believe that God gave us intelligence, common sense and fear to keep us out of scary and dangerous situations, it couldn't hurt. God does seem to love fools—there are certainly plenty of us—and we keep developing new ways of proving our stupidity.

THE END

For the most part, the Civil War ghosts of north Georgia are where you would expect to find them: at Chickamauga and sites of vicious combat along the route of the Atlanta Campaign. The spirits remain at places where they served and died, on battlefields and in a wide variety of buildings used as hospitals, as well as the homes they returned to and where lived out their lives, their distinguished military services never far from their minds. Civil War ghosts experienced in Georgia seem to be increasing due to substantial encroachment on battlefields; renovations to antebellum structures, which ghosts dislike intensely; and the growing number of people searching out paranormal phenomena, scientifically and otherwise.

In closing, I would like to quote Joshua Chamberlain of the Twentieth Maine, a hero of Gettysburg, who wrote decades after the war, "In great deeds, something abides. On great fields, something stays. Forms change and pass; bodies disappear; but spirits linger, to consecrate ground for the vision-place of souls."

APPENDIX

HAUNTED PLACES OPEN TO THE PUBLIC

Listed in order as they appear in text.

Chickamauga and Chattanooga National Military Park
P.O. Box 2128, Fort Oglethorpe, GA 30742
(706) 866-9241; fax (423) 752-5215
http://www.nps.gov/chch/index.htm

Gordon-Lee Mansion
217 Cove Road, Chickamauga, GA 30707
(706) 375-4728; (706) 375-9499
http://www.gordonleemansion.com
rbarclift@cityofchickamauga.org

Western & Atlantic Railroad Tunnel Heritage Center Museum
215 Clisby Austin Road, Tunnel Hill, GA 30755
(706) 876-1571
http://www.tunnelhillheritagecenter.com

Friends of Resaca
P.O. Box 1098, Resaca, GA 30375
(706) 602-2224
www.resacabattlefield.org

Barnsley Gardens Resorts
597 Barnsley Gardens Road, Adairsville, GA 30103
(770) 773-7480; (877) 773-2447
www.barnsleyresort.com

Etowah Valley Historical Society
115 West Cherokee Avenue, P.O. Box 1886, Cartersville, GA 30120
(770) 606-8862
http://evhsonline.org/bartow-history/civil-war
evhs@evhsonline.org

Paulding County Historical Society and Museum
295 North Johnston Street, P.O. Box 333, Dallas, GA 30132
(678) 318-1394
http://www.pchsm.org
pchsminc@gmail.com

Pickett's Mill Battlefield State Historic Site
4432 Mount Tabor Road, Dallas, GA 30157
(770) 443-7850
www.pickettsmillpark.org

Longstreet Society
P.O. Box 191, Gainesville, GA
and
Piedmont Hotel
827 Maple Street, Gainesville, GA
(770) 539-9005
http://www.longstreetsociety.org

Callaway Plantation
2160 Lexington Road (U.S. 78 five miles west of Washington), Washington, GA 30673
(706) 678-7060

Robert Toombs House Historic Site
216 Robert Toombs Avenue, Washington, GA 30673
(706) 678-2226
http://gastateparks.org/RobertToombsHouse?mode=m&p=47Georgia

Georgia Regents University/U.S. Arsenal
1120 Fifteenth Street, Augusta, GA 30912
(706) 721-0211
http://www.gru.edu

Demosthenian Society
Demosthenian Hall (Old North Campus, College Street), University of Georgia, Athens, GA 30602
demosthenian@gmail.com

T.R.R. Cobb House
175 Hill Street, Athens, GA 30601-2419
(706) 369-3513; fax (706) 354-1054
www.trrcobbhouse.org
info@trrcobbhouse.org

Ghost Tours

Ghost tours have been a popular form of historical entertainment for many years, and they often incorporate paranormal tales relating to the Civil War. Roswell has an established tour, and other cities occasionally sponsor them. Ghost tour operators, like ghost hunting organizations, rise and fall frequently, so check to see what is currently available in your area of interest, particularly around Halloween.

Bibliography

Alan, Ian. *Georgia Ghosts: They Are Among Us.* Birmingham, AL: Sweetwater Press, 2005.

Asfar, Dan, and Edrick That. *Ghost Stories of the Civil War.* Alberta, Canada: Ghost House Books, 2003.

Belanger, Jeff. *Ghosts of War: Restless Spirits of Soldiers, Spies, and Saboteurs.* Franklin Lakes, NJ: New Page Books, 2006.

Bender, William N. *Haunted Atlanta and Beyond.* Toccoa, GA: Currahee Books, 2008.

Blackmarr, Amy. *Dahlonega Haunts: Ghostly adventures in a Georgia Mountain Town.* Albany, GA: Willacoochee Publishing Company, 2005.

Blue & Gray Magazine's Guide to Haunted Places of the Civil War. Columbus, OH: Blue & Gray Magazine and The General's Books, 1996.

Brown, Alan. *Ghost Hunters of the South.* Jackson: University Press of Mississippi, 2006.

———. *Haunted Georgia: Ghosts and Strange Phenomena of the Peach State.* Mechanicsburg, PA: Stackpole Books, 2008.

———. *Stories from the Haunted South.* Jackson: University Press of Mississippi, 2004.

Coleman, Christopher, K. *Ghosts and Haunts of the Civil War.* Nashville, TN: Rutledge Hill Press, 1999.

———. *Strange Tales of the Dark and Bloody Ground.* Nashville, TN: Rutledge Hill Press, 1998.

Duffey, Barbara. *Angels and Apparitions: True Ghost Stories from the South.* Eatonton, GA: Elysian Publishing Company, 1996.

———. *Banshees, Bugles and Belles: True Georgia Ghost Stories*. Berryville, VA: Rockbridge Publishing Company, 1999.

———. *Miracles from Heaven*. Eatonton, GA: Elysian Publishing Company, 1998.

Glass, Debra, and Heath Mathews. *Skeletons of the Civil War: True Ghost Stories of the Army of Tennessee*. 2007. Florence, AL: Debra Johnston.

Kotarski, Georgiana C. *Ghosts of the Southern Tennessee Valley*. Winston-Salem, NC: John F. Blair Publishers, 2006.

Miles, Jim. *Civil War Sites in Georgia*. Nashville, TN: Rutledge Hill Press, 1996.

———. *Fields of Glory*. Nashville, TN: Cumberland House, 2002.

———. *Weird Georgia*. New York: Sterling, 2007.

Mooney, Diane S. "Lost but Now Found, Soldiers Graves Uncovered at Clayton-Mooney House." *Etowah Valley Historical Society Newsletter*, September 1994.

Perkerson, Medora Field. *White Columns in Georgia*. New York City: Rinehart & Company, 1952.

Reevy, Tony, ed. *Ghost Train! American Railroad Ghost Stories*. Lynchburg, VA: TLC Publishing Inc., 2002.

Roberts, Nancy. *Georgia Ghosts*. Winston-Salem, NC: John F. Blair, Publisher, 1997.

Sallee, Scott E., ed. "Camp Talk." *Blue & Gray* 18, no. 1 (October 2000).

Sanders, Michael. *Strange Tales of the Civil War*. Shippensburg, PA: Burd Street Press, 2001.

Smith, Gordon Burns, and Anna Habersham Wright Smith. *Ghost Dances and Shadow Pantomimes: Eyewitness Accounts of the Supernatural from Old Georgia*. Vol. 1. Milledgeville, GA: Boyd Publishing, 2004.

Spaeth, Frank, ed. *Phantom Army of the Civil War*. Secaucus, NJ: Castle Books, 1997.

Taylor, Troy. *Spirits of the Civil War*. Alton, IL: Whitechapel Productions Press, 1999.

Toney, B. Keith. *Battlefield Ghosts*. Berryville, VA: Rockbridge Publishing, 1997.

Turnage, Sheila. *Haunted Inns of the Southeast*. Winston-Salem, NC: John F. Blair, 2001.

Underwood, Corinna. *Haunted History: Atlanta and North Georgia*. Atglen, PA: Schiffer Publishing, 2008.

Visions of Ghost Armies: Real-Life Encounters with War-Torn Spirits, from the Files of FATE *Magazine*. New York City: Barnes & Noble, 2003.

Walls, Kathleen. *Georgia's Ghostly Getaways*. N.p.: Global Authors Publications, 2003.

Wangler, Chris. *Ghost Stories of Georgia: True Tales of Ghostly Hauntings*. Auburn, WA: Long Pine Publishing International, 2006.

Winer, Richard, and Nancy Osborn Ishmael. *Haunted Houses*. New York: Bantam, 1979.

———. *More Haunted Houses*. New York City: Bantam, 1983.

WEBSITES

Foundation for Paranormal Research. http://www.foundationforparanormalresearch.org.

The Moonlit Road. http://themoonlitroad.com.

About the Author

Jim Miles is author of seven books of the Civil War Explorer Series (*Fields of Glory*, *To the Sea*, *Piercing the Heartland*, *Paths to Victory*, *A River Unvexed*, *Forged in Fire* and *The Storm Tide*), *Civil War Sites in Georgia* and two books titled *Weird Georgia*. Five books were featured by the History Book Club, and he has been historical adviser to two History Channel documentaries. He has a bachelor's degree in history and a Master of Education degree from Georgia Southwestern State University in Americus. He taught high school American history for thirty-one years. Over a span of forty years, Jim has logged tens of thousands of miles exploring literally every nook and cranny in Georgia, as well as Civil War sites throughout the country. He lives in Warner Robins, Georgia, with his wife, Earline.